Ritual and Secrecy Confront Reality

Also from Westphalia Press

westphaliapress.org

Ritual and Secrecy Confront Reality

Volume 2, Number 1 of Ritual, Secrecy and Civil Society

Edited by Pierre Mollier

WESTPHALIA PRESS
An imprint of Policy Studies Organization

Ritual and Secrecy Confront Reality: Volume 2, Number 1 of Ritual, Secrecy and Civil Society
All Rights Reserved © 2014 by Policy Studies Organization

Westphalia Press
An imprint of Policy Studies Organization
1527 New Hampshire Ave., NW
Washington, D.C. 20036
info@ipsonet.org

ISBN-13: 978-1-63391-117-8
ISBN-10: 1633911179

Cover design by Taillefer Long at Illuminated Stories:
www.illuminatedstories.com

Daniel Gutierrez-Sandoval, Executive Director
PSO and Westphalia Press

Rahima Schwenkbeck, Director of Media and Marketing
PSO and Westphalia Press

Updated material and comments on this edition
can be found at the Westphalia Press website:
www.westphaliapress.org

Table of Contents

Ritual, Secrecy, and Civil Society:
Volume 2, Number 1, Spring 2014

Freemasonry, Enlightenment, and Networks

Foreword by Pierre Mollier

Although Anglo-Saxon Freemasonry has always claimed that it "does not do politics," Latin Freemasonries in Europe or South America have in fact helped to promote new, liberal, and progressive ideas. Historians must look beyond the official discourse and study the interactions between the often important organizations of the Grand Lodges and the societies to which they belong.

Building on the works of Margaret Jacob, our first two articles examine the political ideas implemented and promoted by the Grand Orient in France in the eighteenth century. We will see very clearly how Masonic dignitaries applied the liberal and predemocratic principles of Enlightenment thinkers in the management of the Lodges under their leadership, even if this often meant going against the opinions and prejudices of "ordinary" Masons. What makes this even more interesting is its occurrence at a time when the leadership of the Grand Orient belonged to the country's ruling classes, and when France was highly influential throughout Europe. Moreover, Masonry was an effective network for exchange in Enlightenment Europe, as shown by the study on the Masons Knights of Malta. We can perceive a new sociability (Freemasonry) relaying and challenging an old sociability (the Order of Malta). It is therefore appropriate to examine the existence of a true geopolitics of Freemasonry in the eighteenth century.

What makes the eighteenth century so interesting to us is that it was one of the key periods in Western culture in terms of literature and the arts, as well as the time when the ideas and values that many still consider to be ours today took shape. Modern man looks to the eighteenth century as a reference point in a similar way to how men in the sixteenth and seventeenth centuries looked to antiquity. This makes it particularly important to examine the role of Freemasonry in this process.

Finally, after a look at these essentially very "European" issues, we include Carter Charles' fascinating study on a very "American" subject: the "Masonic" sources of certain aspects of the Mormon religion.

Welcome to our third issue—a number of great symbolic significance for Freemasons! It shows that Ritual, Secrecy, and Civil Society has now fully secured its place among academic journals on Freemasonry and fraternalism.

Pierre Mollier
Editor-in-Chief

Election, Representation, and Democracy: Debates Surrounding the Organization of the Grand Orient de France (1773-1789)

Pierre Mollier[1]

The position of the lodges during the Enlightenment and the French Revolution is a classic question in the eighteenth-century historiography. Initially denounced by certain counterrevolutionaries, the connection of Freemasonry to the events of 1789–1793 was later claimed by the Republican Brothers at the end of the nineteenth century. However, from Mathiez to Alain Le Bihan and Pierre Chevallier, the professional historians of the twentieth century ultimately challenged the idea that Freemasonry had played any real role in the revolutionary storm, dismissing the lodges as simple societies of banquets and festivities. The debate has been taken up again over the last 20 years with the works of Ran Halévy[2] and Margaret Jacob.[3] According to slightly different modalities, both give it an important role in the implementation and spread of a democratic social practice that prepared the way for political modernity. Thus, in *Living the Enlightenment*, Margaret Jacob emphasizes all the work the lodges undertook concerning their own organization. She shows how a group's collective reflection concerning the authority it submits to and the rules it applies to itself signal a different conception of public space and thus dissimulates a social work that is in fact political. Her research is based on a series of case studies in several European countries, and critics have at times underscored the selective nature of her examples. Thus *a contrario*, how can we analyze the phenomenon of the Templar Strict Observance, if not as a reaction by the nobility, which would seem to be a far cry from any democratic learning process? In this article, we would like to examine an episode of French Masonic history during which the success of the concept of "democratic social practice" seems particularly ripe for analysis. It involves debates on the statutes and rules of the Grand Orient de France that took place in Paris between 1773 and 1789. This study of a case which until now has remained in the shadows offers several advantages. First, it does not simply involve one Masonic group among others, but is the reflection of a body that brought together almost all French Freemasons. Second, throughout those 20 years, the officials of the Grand Orient would be led to clarify, modify, and make changes to these internal rules depending on the circumstances. We are thus able to witness how a collective rule is debated and constructed over time during the last decades of the *Ancien Régime*. Finally, since all of the archives have been preserved, we have a very large set of documents on the development of rules

---

[1] Pierre Mollier, Director of the Grand Orient de France Library and of the Museum of Freemasonry (Paris).

[2] Ran Halévi, *Les Loges maçonniques dans la France d'Ancien Régime aux origines de la sociabilité démocratique* (Paris: Cahier des Annales, Librairie Armand Colin, 1984).

[3] Margaret C. Jacob, *Living the Enlightenment, Freemasonry and Politics in Eighteenth-century Europe* (New York/Oxford: Oxford University Press, 1991).

as well as on their later implementation in the different bodies. An additional interest, aside from the persons and individual futures in the *bourgeoisie de robe*s or the liberal nobility, is that the officials of the Grand Orient undoubtedly belonged to the social classes that would launch the Revolution. Given the breadth of the topic, in this article we will limit ourselves to drawing attention to this veritable mine for historiography, present points of reference, and suggest a few directions for future work.

1728–1773: French Masonic Authority Struggles to Organize

From its introduction to Paris around 1725 until the end of the 1760s, French Freemasonry would repeatedly endeavor to organize itself. It first recognized the authority of a Grand Master for France in 1728,[4] thereby freeing itself from English tutelage. In 1735, it endowed itself with statutes, establishing a Grand Lodge for the first time.[5] However, this First Grand Lodge did not seem to hold much authority over the lodges of the Kingdom. At regular intervals—June 24, 1745; July 4, 1755; May 19, 1760; and April 17, 1763[6] —it would try to establish its supremacy by promulgating statutes. Each of these texts insists on the authority it claims to have over the lodges of the kingdom, but to little effect. Until the

1760s, the lodges existed in semi-independence. Older lodges established newer ones and each corresponded with various others, depending on the circumstances. The unity of French Freemasonry could only be found in the fact that all recognized the Grand Master. From 1743 to 1771, he would be a prominent figure in Louis XV's France, namely, the Count of Clermont, a *prince du sang*. However, the rule of Louis de Bourbon-Condé was only a symbolic patronage and relatively distant, as was the custom during the *Ancien Régime*; the Grand Master never intervened in the management of the Order. It was, however, in his name that, in 1761, the first real attempt was made to establish a central authority over the lodges. Through a substitute appointed by the Grand Master, Augustin Chaillon de Jonville, the Grand Lodge came to life and the lodges of the kingdom were informed that they would then have to pledge allegiance to it. However, the "awoken" Grand Lodge was populated solely by Parisians, and the provinces complained about recognizing the "Grand Lodge of Masters of Paris said to be of France,[7] according to the brothers from Lyon. It was challenged and quickly split into different factions, and again interrupted its work in 1766. The death of the Count of Clermont in 1771 and the need to elect a successor brought about a new meeting of the Grand Lodge.

---

[4] See Alain Le Bihan, "Paris: 1728, Les maçons et les Grands Maîtres jacobites ou la reconnaissance du premier d'entre eux: le Duc de Wharton," in *Les plus belles pages de la Franc-maçonnerie française* (Paris: Dervy, 2003), 36-37.

[5] See Etienne Fournial, *Les plus anciens devoirs et règlements de la Franc-maçonnerie française, Annales du Grand Orient de France—Supplément au n°48 du Bulletin du G∴O∴X de France* (Paris: n.p., 1964); new edition, *Renaissance Traditionnelle* 134 (April 2003).

[6] These texts are published in: *Alain Le Bihan, Francs-maçons et ateliers parisiens de la Grande Loge de France au XVIIIe siècle (1760–1795)* (Paris: Bibliothèque Nationale, 1973).

[7] BnF, FM¹ 111 a, folio 35, cited by René Désagulliers in "La Grande Loge de Paris dite de France et les "autres grades" de 1756 à 1766," *Renaissance Traditionnelle* 89 (January 1992): 14.

The Formation of the Grand Orient: A Crisis in Representation?

The events that would lead to the formation of the Grand Orient de France thus begin like a classic episode of the *Ancien Régime*—with the gathering of notable figures to solicit a protector—and would in a few weeks be transformed into a "National Assembly" of elected deputies.[8] After the death of the Count of Clermont, a minority faction of the former Grand Lodge attempted to reestablish its audience and skillfully offered the leadership of the order to the Duke of Montmorency-Luxembourg. It was also agreed that the Grand Mastership would be offered to the Duke of Chartre, cousin of the King, future head of the house of Orléans and thus the noble with the highest rank in the kingdom after his father; a candidate who could not be contested. He accepted, which made any real opposition to the process that began impossible. It would be delayed, however, for a few months due to the momentary disgrace of Philippe d'Orléans, who was removed from the Court for opposing parliamentary reform. Parisian Masonic circles began to agitate and a group reunited around the new "Administrator General" (such is the title adopted by the Duke of Montmorency-Luxembourg) proposed a long list of reforms to finally give French Freemasonry a truly shared organization.

The main obstacle remained the majority faction of the former Grand Lodge that was not associated with these events. Montmorency-Luxembourg's entire strategy would be to marginalize it by challenging its representativeness; traditional authority would be countered with representative authority. For this, principles would be proposed whose application would go well beyond the scope of Freemasonry. The replacement of officials and the implementation of a new Masonic administration implied the adoption of new statutes. The rules of 1763 appeared obsolete and the former Grand Lodge had itself changed its reference texts several times. New statutes were thus prepared by a commission in close collaboration with Montmorency-Luxembourg. Officially, of course, it was simply a question of *"reforming abuses returning the royal art to its former splendor and luster."*[9] The challenge for the different assemblies would be to adopt these new statutes which would validate the reform orchestrated by the Administrator General. Beginning in Chapter 1, two articles point to a small revolution in terms of the customs of the former Grand Lodge. Article 4 of Section 1 states: *"The Grand Orient de France will forthwith only recognize as Lodge Worshipful Master [president] the Master raised to this rank by the free choice of the Members of the Lodge."* This marked the end of the "irremovable" Worshipful Master who held their presidency "for life," which was how any particular office was held at the time. Election became the norm and would be applied to all Masonic functions. The Grand Master and the Administrator General set the example by vacating their initial

---

[8] For a presentation that is both specific and inclusive of the fairly complex process that would lead to the formation of the Grand Orient de France, see Pierre Chevallier, *Histoire de la Franc-maçonnerie, I—La Maçonnerie Ecole de l'Egalité (1725–1799)* (Paris: Fayard, 1974), 151–176. To follow the details of these operations see *Constitution du Grand Orient de France par la Grande Loge Nationale*—1773, introduction by Arthur Groussier (Paris: Gloton, 1931), which transcribes all the minutes of the meetings and several appendices; and Daniel Kerjan, *Les Débuts de la franc-maçonnerie française, de la Grande Loge au Grand Orient, 1688–1793* (Paris: Devy, 2013).

[9] Assembly of known deputies of the LL∴ of Province on March 8, 1773 in *Constitution du Grand Orient de France*, 47.

appointment by the officials of the Grand Lodge, and by presenting themselves for election, bringing together representatives from all the lodges. Not only did the Administrator General, the First Christian Baron of France, submit to the election, but he also agreed to enter into the debate arena with the good bourgeois of the former Grand Lodge, who were decided to ask high price for their sacrifice. The second key innovation: "*The Grand Orient de France shall be constituted of [...] all the current Worshipful Master or Deputies of the Lodges, both in Paris and in the Provinces*" (Chapter 1, Section 2, Article 1). All the lodges would thus be represented in the new administration of the Order. Seeing that they were offered a share of power, the delegates of the provincial lodges, who had been somewhat distrustful at first, in the end rallied to the reform and became its main supporters. The members from Lyon who 10 years earlier had chastised "*the Grand Lodge of the Masters of Paris said to be of France*" hailed the "*National Assembly*"[10] of Lodges. This expression was used several times during the discussions in Paris. The debates, followed by the gradual adoption of the new statutes by the deputies of the lodges in Paris and the provinces, established the legitimacy of the new Grand Orient and the authority of the Duke of Montmorency-Luxembourg over the Order. It also gave French Freemasonry a new organization. The "Government of the Order" depended on three chambers: the Chamber of Administration, the Chamber of Paris, and the Chamber of the Provinces. As their names suggest, the first guaranteed the management of the

central organization and especially finances, while the other two managed the lodges in terms of their respective constituencies (Constitutions, certificates, various disputes...). The members of these bodies were all elected from within the assembly of the deputies of the lodges because:

> "*The forty-five current officers shall always be up for the election of the Grand Orient; one-third shall be renewed every year [...] and chosen in the Grand Orient.*"[11]

In a few months, these meetings bringing together representatives of the enlightened bourgeoisie—such as Lalande or Guillotin—and the liberal nobility—such as Montmorency-Luxembourg and his friends—would set up an organization that was radically different from the former Grand Lodge. Principles in place at the new Grand Orient de France, such as the relative separation of powers,[12] elections, and representation at all levels, were no doubt inspired by the ideas of the Enlightenment which were for the first time applied within the eighteenth-century France. Pierre Chevallier shrewdly remarked:

> "*The Masonic Constituent Assembly that was the National Grand Lodge would end its sessions on September 1, 1773. Without seeking to make an excessive comparison with the General Assemblies of 1789, one cannot, however, help but take note of the similarities that reveal a shared mindset.*"[13]

---

[10] Letter from the lodges of Lyon to their deputy Bacon de la Chevalerie, *Constitution du Grand Orient de France*, 174.

[11] Statute of the Royal Order of Freemasonry, Chapter 2, Section 2, Article 1, in *Constitution du Grand Orient de France*, 238.

[12] Finally, we could also point out the decisions concerning the different chambers, especially in matters of dispute, by a "Managing Board."

[13] Chevallier, *Histoire de la Franc-maçonnerie*, 166.

The "Democratic" Life of the Grand Orient from 1773 to 1793

Texts are one thing, but practices are something else. How would these "statutes of the Enlightenment" be applied in the daily operation of the Grand Orient? Numerous registers of the minutes of the various bodies of the Order show that the dignitaries really played the game of their liberal, predemocratic rules. There are many examples, but here are just a few. At the opening of the assembly of the Grand Orient that took place 10 times a year, the president asks:

> "...whether some deputies [have] requests to make for the LL∴ they represent."[14]

Persons regularly had to be appointed to vacant positions and the election always seemed fairly open. Such was the case on May 19, 1786, for the important positions of First Grand Surveillants:

> "The T∴C∴F∴ Duke de Crussol was appointed by a plurality of twenty-eight votes, the V∴F∴ Marquis de Vichy received six, and the F∴ Count de Roure one. Three were found to be blank."[15]

The nobility, dukes, marquis, and counts submitted to the election of Brothers Sue, Carrel, Martin, Robin, etc.—all bourgeois.

As "policy" documents, the statutes of 1773 first aimed at unifying the lodges around a few principles and a new team. In the daily existence of the association, over the years and as problems arose, a certain number of clarifications would have to be made to the operations of the bodies of the Order. The chambers of the Grand Orient were thus led to develop supplementary rules. All these regulatory changes were not simply technical adjustments—far from it. Thus, beginning in 1775, it was decided that the two main leaders of the Grand Orient, the Administrator General and the Grand Conservator, would be subject to election: previously, the individuals in these roles had held them permanently once initially elected. In addition, in the very language of the article, it was emphasized that the point was to reintegrate them into the common law. Thus, they are *"removable after 3 years and their appointment will be carried out in the same way as the other officers of the G.O."*[16] In a magnanimous gesture, the Grand Master himself would offer to renounce his irremovability and also be subject to election every three years, but the Brothers refused.

For the vote to be fair, it had to be done in full knowledge of the facts, so during the 122nd assembly of the Grand Orient —February 15, 1782—it was decided after the debates that all deputies of the lodges would be able to ask for disclosures from the secretariat of the Grand Orient.[17] Also, all the members would have access to the files, as long as they were commissioned by a lodge. It was also decided that, as far as possible, agendas would always be announced ahead of time. One subject that would occupy the bodies of the association for a long time was the establishment of a specific procedure for electing the officers

---

[14] For example, during the 162nd assembly of the G∴O∴ on August 19, 1785, BnF FM¹ 16, folio 181.

[15] 169th assembly of the G∴O∴, May 19, 1786, BnF FM¹ 16, folio 251, back.

[16] FM¹ 98, folio 11, back.

[17] 122nd assembly of the G∴O∴, February 15, 1782, BnF FM¹ 16, folio 186, back.

of the different chambers. Indeed, they were the ones who, with the assistance of the secretariat, ensured the daily administration of the Grand Orient, which indicates the importance of the challenge. In August 1785, the voting procedure was presented in great detail:

"The first expert shall count the voters and shall give to each a ballot. Each voter shall write on this ballot the name, surname, statuses, age, and residence of the brother he believes should be nominated. The first expert shall collect the ballots. The Brothers who have no one to nominate shall submit blank ballots. The ballots shall be given to the President who shall count them in the presence of two experts. If the number of ballots is not equal to the number of voters, the operation shall begin again. The President shall open the ballots and shall read what they contain. The ballots that nominate the same names shall be gathered and there shall be as many stacks as there are different names. Each stack shall be counted and the President shall appoint all the Brothers nominated beginning with the one who received the most votes...."[18]

Is this not an example of the learning process of democracy? Several other examples of procedural votes of this kind can be found in the internal rules of the Grand Orient. But we should be wary of models that seem too perfect. While they focus much attention on the rigor of the elective procedure, the managers of the Grand Orient simultaneously try to limit access to the offices by introducing some measure of

cooptation. This raises the opposition of the Brother Desjunquières who argues against:

"...the rule of August 17, 1785 [which] tends to completely separate the officers of the Grand Orient from the deputies of the lodges and make it a distinct body. I have never considered the Grand Orient except as the lodge of deputies who have the right to elect from within it, officers to preside over, conduct, and clarify the work, as well as administrate more specifically the Order's affairs and prepare the documents to be brought before the G. O."[19]

Tellingly, the examples he then gives to legitimize respect for the democratic spirit are classic cases of the most traditional social practices of the Ancien Régime:

"If we want to take civil societies as a model, nothing exists any longer or nothing comparable is practiced unless we look to the first finance companies or to the latest corporations of arts and crafts."

This shows how the connections between traditional and new social practices were more complex than the simple opposition of ancient and modern! Brother Desjunquière's argument won the day and the rule that had been approved was annulled. All the deputies from the lodges at the Grand Orient became again eligible for the various offices. What is interesting about this episode is that it illustrates the complexity of the development of this new democratic social practice and also shows how it is connected to older forms of social

---

[18] Archives of the GODF, BnF FM¹ 16, folio 246.

[19] Archives of the GODF, BnF FM¹ 16, folio 247.

relationships. The 15 years between the formation of the Grand Orient and 1789 would witness several similar episodes. In each case, the details of the debates, the constant back and forth between the various bodies, and the frequent repetitions all make the reading of these long minutes particularly tedious. Nevertheless, our hope is that eighteenth-century specialists will take note of how relevant the documentation contained in the archives of the Grand Orient of France is for the study of the formation of democratic social practices in the years preceding the Revolution.

During the early days of 1789, the Grand Orient sent a circular to all the lodges it corresponded with to report on its activity. The introduction of this text is particularly interesting. It reads:

> "*Enlightened concerning their true interests, the LL∴ felt it necessary to be governed in a uniform way, and to submit to rules drawn from the very essence of their association: this motive led them to unite to form a common center, and they decreed that the body that would regulate them would be composed of their representatives; therefore, they attributed legislative power to this body, and established it as judge of their differences.*
> *The constitution of the G∴O∴, TT∴C-C∴FF∴, is thus purely democratic: nothing shall be decided except according to the will of the LLs∴, brought before the General Assemblies by their representatives.*"

Of course, the general atmosphere that began to affect French society at the beginning of 1789 may not be entirely absent from what was written here; but it can clearly be concluded that this text was in line with what had been the doctrine of the Grand Orient since 1773.

---

[20] Circular of the 19th day of the eleventh month 5788 (January 19, 1789).

The Ideological Foundations of the Grand Orient de France

Daniel Kerjan[1]

The success of the Grand Orient de France in the eighteenth century is not solely due to the solidness of the institution established in 1773: there were 115 active lodges in 1774, 656 in 1789, close to 100 Chapters instituted by the General Grand Chapter or the Metropolitan Sovereign Chapter. These three figures, more persuasively than any long discussion, reveal the success of Freemasonry that Montmorency-Luxemburg was seeking and which the Grand Orient de France embodied. They raise a question: What were the reasons for such success, which resulted in the Obedience's quasi-hegemony in the kingdom's masonic landscape? The reasons are in fact multiple: a policy of active communication; strict financial management; the annual renewal of Venerables, which was emulated in the workshops; the effective representation of provincial lodges at the Paris board through deputies; the presence of freemasons in places of power; and the incorporation of high ranks of the French rite into the system's institution.

Its ideological relevance and permanence would also give it strength, by drawing in a growing number of individual members. Gathering men together, regardless of their condition or convictions, is the first goal of Freemasonry. Even though at the end of the eighteenth century, there was a strong philosophical trend that supported such an attitude, it was rejected by the Catholic Church, which refused to compromise the "true faith" and thus fought against any other faith. It was also rejected by the tenets of an omnipresent social or racial determinism within Ancien Regime society. It was thus from within that the Grand Orient would have to endeavor to change minds.

The Rejection of Exclusions

The first attitude adopted by the Grand Orient that distinguished it from all other institutions that existed at the time was the rejection of exclusions related to religious belief. Thus on May 15, 1786, the F∴ Louis Salivet, orator of the Chamber of the Provinces of the Grand Orient sent the following letter to the "La Parfaite" lodge of Nancy:

It has been reported to us that an Algerian mason, the F∴ Méhémet Célibi, finding himself at your Orient, presented himself to gain entry to your temple. We were informed that this brother was met with a refusal on your part. Such conduct seemed to us to contain secret motives which were not communicated to us.

Steeped as we are in the principles that all Masons are part of the same family, we were surprised, TT∴C-C∴FF∴, that a difference of religion was the pretext you used to turn away

---

[1] Daniel Kerjan, Member of the Institut d'Etudes et de Recherches Maçonniques (IDERM)

the Algerian brother. You know that there is no Masonic text that does not present our society as a people of brothers whose first duty is to love and mutually help one another regardless of one's religion. The first religion of a Mason is humanity. This is very unlike anything invented by fanaticism that seeks to distance men from each other and inspire horror in them for their fellow men! It is up to Freemasonry to provide an example of tolerance, to seek out the Scythian, the Lapplander, the African and all others who live in this world, to show them there are no differences between men, aside from their feelings and their way of life.

Our Order, TT∴CC∴FF∴, in working to bring about this positive reconciliation, may be called The Institution of Nature: it is not sufficient that this vow be continually upon our lips, but even more must our hearts realize it by actions worthy of it. Is there anything better than restoring man to his primary condition, by persuading the most powerful that the weakest is his brother? We therefore invite you to share with us the reasons why you did not receive into your circle the F∴Méhémet Célébi, and we ask that you would explain why with the frankness characteristic of true Masons. This enlightenment is necessary so that we can decide on the welcome this foreign brother deserves to receive in the workshops we correspond with, should he present himself to visit them.[2]

The case of this Algerian Brother remains marginal, however, since the number of Muslim merchants from North Africa that might have been received at a lodge is cer-

tainly quite limited. Such was not the case with brothers of the Jewish faith. It was thus that in 1783 "La Zélée," at Bayonne, saw its Venerable Casemajor, lawyer and prosecutor of La Prévôté, as well as many of its members, withdraw and found another lodge, "L'Amitié." Antisemitism was the unique cause of this split:

In the principle of its creation, La Zélée had been fairly unscrupulous in choosing its members. Among others, it had let in many Jews who, in this country, are excluded from any honest society, and who presented themselves en masse in this lodge when it began. This reception hindered many brothers, who were respected due to their civil qualities, to present themselves as members. We felt the need to separate ourselves from these Jews, and we were happy to do so.[3]

Such ostracism was, however, strongly contested by the Grand Orient, as demonstrated by this call to order addressed to the "Enfants de l'Union Triomphante" at Castelnaudary in 1778:

According to article 73 of your particular Regulation you forbid any Jewish Mason, even if they have a certificate, from entering your workshop. The fundamental regulations of our Order expressly prohibit us in the lodges from concerning ourselves with anything foreign to Freemasonry. Therefore, a Freemason should not inquire concerning the beliefs of a brother who can prove, with authentic documents, that he has been initiated into the Order, and that he still holds to the feelings that granted him this favor.[4]

---

[2] Correspondence of the Chamber of the Provinces, FM1 87 a.

[3] FM[1] 159 a, letter of July 12, 1783 from Casemajor to the Grand Orient.

[4] FM[1] 86, Correspondence of the Chamber of the Provinces with the lodges, June 5, 1778.

However, prejudice was such that the issue of admitting Jews would continue to be raised and in 1789 again, the Grand Orient's position would have to be reaffirmed.

Any man who has the morals, conduct, and character required by the statutes of the Order may be accepted into the mysteries of the Royal Art, and therefore the lodge may receive Jews when it recognizes in them the qualities that constitute a true Mason.[5]

The issue was also raised when it involved persons with mixed blood:

You are seeking to know whether or not you can give the light to two American laymen, gifted with all the necessary qualities to become good masons. The birth of these two subjects is the reason why two members of your R∴L∴ have doubts concerning their possible admission, because they have a white father and a black mother.

This objection will disappear by consulting the vow of nature that makes all men equal. But there is another consideration that resolves the problem. In France, all men are free, and based on this unique reason, the condition of their mother cannot be put forward as an argument against the candidates. The two laymen in question seem to us to be completely worthy, such that the members of your R∴L∴ who are undecided should not be held back by the consideration that caused them to doubt. There is no regulation that excludes those who find themselves in the same situation as these Americans.[6]

Blacks, however, continued to be excluded. The issue was only raised in the colonies, but in order to obtain the constitution of his lodge, as requested on December 25, 1789, Brother Lislet, a black Creole, had to withdraw from the "Les Quinze Artistes" lodge at Port-Louis, Ile de France (Maurice Island), owing to the opposition of the Provincial Grand Lodge of the Island of Bourbon (La Réunion). "*The custom is to not admit any Blacks into either civil or masonic societies.*" The universal vocation of the Grand Orient's Freemasonry is nevertheless clearly affirmed in a letter dated October 2, 1786 to the "La Sagesse" lodge of Portsmouth, in Virginia, following a request for affiliation this workshop sent to Paris:

All the masons in the universe should form a single society, if all are to be conducted according to the same principles. But the variety of regimes that have been instituted among them has caused there to be in every kingdom, among every people, almost as many republics that govern themselves according to specific laws. However, all these small Masonic states have a single goal, which is to honor virtue and assist their fellow man. The need to refine Freemasonry in France, and the even greater need to end the kind of abjection into which it had fallen, gave birth to our establishment. We have to believe that the measures we have taken to raise it out of its degradation, and our vigilance to maintain it in this state of honesty and decency were worth of our consideration, since

---

[5] FM¹ 19, Recording of the minutes of the Symbolic Chamber, response to "La Parfaite Union" at Montauban, January 7, 1789.

[6] FM¹ 86, December 15, 1788, letter to "L'Indulgente Amitié" of Barbezieux.

the existence of our establishment has spread even to your lands. It is no doubt the esteem you give to it that we owe the request you addressed to us, to be united at the common center of French Freemasonry.[7]

Starting in 1774, the Chamber of Administration also affirmed that "*the title of foreigner is not an obstacle for taking up eminent positions while this foreigner resides in France.*"[8] The most famous beneficiary of this arrangement would be Benjamin Franklin, who enjoyed the title of Venerable of "Les Neuf Soeurs" lodge between 1778 and 1779, during his stay in Paris. Also, during the uprising that troubled the Netherlands beginning in 1785, during which King William V fled to England, the brothers of "Amitié et Fraternité" at Dunkirk were asked to warmly welcome the exiles:

The events that forced a large number of Dutch masons to expatriate themselves should be a further reason for French masons to welcome them. The fact that most of them were unable to bring their Masonic certificates because of their rapid flight due to the troubles in their homeland should not be an obstacle barring them entry to your Temple. It is enough to take the necessary precautions to ensure to what point they have been initiated into our mysteries. Once certain of the knowledge of the Royal Art, you can receive them into your circles without fear.[9]

Clearly, the Grand Orient opposed any form of exclusion related to nationality, religion, or the color of one's skin. It went even further:

Can a man deprived of sight be initiated into our mysteries? We will not hide from you that this proposition has been the subject of a lively debate. The difficulty of reception, the fear of exposing our mysteries to the indiscretion of a man whose good faith may be surprised, and especially that he would not perceive the traps that may be set for him, were all motives, among others, that held back the goodwill of a large portion of our brothers. Others, to the contrary, were led by the pleasure of offering some respite to an unfortunate person deprived of the most necessary sense, of lightening his burdens by causing him to enjoy the comforts of brotherhood. The rights of humanity carried the day, and we decided that a man deprived of sight could be initiated into our mysteries.[10]

The Sociological Limits of Brotherhood

However, this desire for openness came up against the prejudices of the day, involving, for example, actors. Thus Bacon de la Chevalerie, Grand Orator during the Summer Festival of the Order of Saint John, celebrated under the presidency of the Grand Master on July 3, 1777, stated on that occasion:

---

[7] FM[1] 87 a, Correspondence of the Chamber of the Provinces to the lodges.

[8] FM[1] 3, Report on the sessions of the Chamber of Administration, March 7, 1774, regarding a disagreement that occurred at the Orient of Mons.

[9] FM[1] 87, Correspondence of the Chamber of the Provinces to the lodges, December 1, 1788.

[9] FM1 13, Correspondence of the Chamber of Administration with the lodges, letter dated December 20, 1782 to "La Parfaite Union" of Agen.

The people intended for public theaters are not recognized by the Grand Orient, not because of the degraded morals attributed to their profession—there are some who may have enough courage to maintain impeccable morals—but because that state causes them to be so dependent on the whims of the public, that often we would be exposed to difficult tests and would be unable to exercise that precious part of our commitment: helping our brothers when they are unjustly humiliated. Prohibition does not include harmony. Could we not respect the flattering and sublime concord of art and nature, which by its melodious and powerful charm animates and supports courage, suspends and consoles pain, maintains or gives birth to the desire to please and the need to love, which is the initial driving force for the formation of societies?[11]

Artists were therefore received reluctantly, and in any case the Grand Orient would not grant them a certificate of Masonic membership. They still had not yet agreed on what the term meant:

Concerning the reasons preventing the two Bedes brothers from becoming members of the La Fidélité lodge at Lectour, we need to know if the sole reason you are opposed is because of the position of artist, and what idea you ascribe to this word in your province. In Paris, an artist is a free-spirited man, and almost always highly regarded: a painter, *an engraver, an architect, these are artists, and there is a significant difference between an artist and an artisan.*[12]

Artisans were also excluded from the Brotherhood. Bacon de la Chevalerie reminds us: *"The exclusion from our mysteries has been declared against all those in the Arts and Crafts who are not Masters. By dismissing a class of purely hired men, the Grand Orient brought together, under its particular viewpoint, the views of the political Government of the Nation and an advantage to Workers: the latter, deprived of a subject of distraction and expense, will, by devoting more time to laboring on their Art, be able to increase their daily subsistence."* The Provincial Grand Lodge at Aix thus recalled the regulation, which specifically said: *"Lodges may admit to the ranks of their members, among the class of citizens called artisans, only masters."* And a later regulation, interpreting the first, adds: *"Rarely should an artisan be accepted, even masters, especially in places where the guilds and communities are not established. Never should workers called* <u>compagnons</u> *in arts and crafts be accepted."*[13] Because they are dependent on a master, they are in effect not free men, an essential quality to become a Freemason. This was also the case for servants, since they also did not have "*a civil status that would allow them to give a few moments to Freemasonry without negatively affecting their daily occupations, and to devote any extra of their fortune to the relief of suffering humanity."*[14]

---

[11] Statement of the Grand Orient, Vol. 1, 4th part.

[12] FM¹ 87, Correspondence of the Chamber of the Provinces, July 29, 1782.

[13] FM¹ 86, September 15, 1788.

[14] FM¹ 86, Letter dated January 3, 1780 to "L'Étoile Polaire," Abbeville and FM1 87 a, Correspondence of the Chamber of the Provinces, letter to "La Vraie Lumière," of Poitiers, March 4, 1782.

Calls to Order

The reception of women into Freemasonry is an issue that still remains to be considered, and would be worth developing separately. Concerning this subject, however, we should recall that women's legal status was the primary obstacle to their integration. Throughout their lives, they remained under the control of the father, and then of the husband. They were thus considered not "free." Aside from these exceptions, the Grand Orient believed in social integration and sought to gather brothers from the nobility, the clergy, as well as the third estate. One of the most interesting characteristics of the period is the active pedagogy that the Grand Orient continued to provide when disputes were sent to it. The workshops were constantly—and fraternally—reminded of very diverse subjects, such as the obligation to be discreet, the principles and practice of Masonic justice, the need to respect regulations or relationships with authorities, etc. It was also through this constant exchange between the Lodges and the Obedience that the Grand Orient was able to establish itself as an ideological reference point with unquestionable moral standards.

Malta, the Knights, and Freemasonry[1]

Pierre Mollier[2]

Formed in London in 1717, over subsequent decades modern Freemasonry spread throughout the whole of eighteenth-century Europe, so quickly and successfully that it still astonishes historians. Its integration and dynamism in Malta, a hub of cultural exchange at the heart of the Mediterranean, is therefore not really surprising, especially given that the young aristocrats who dominated the Order of Saint John (which had many French members) were open to the spirit of their time and particularly to Enlightenment thought. Despite Lodges being condemned by the Pope in 1738, they had many ecclesiastical members in all Catholic countries. The interest of research attempting to improve our understanding of the relationships between Masonry and the Knights of Malta lies not in an apparent paradox (which actually existed not in the eighteenth century), but in the study of the superposition of two networks of sociability, each of which, in its own way, extended over much of Europe. There was a permanent flow of exchange between hundreds of Commanderies of the Order of Saint John in France, Spain, Portugal, Italy, Austria, South Germany... and the Principality of Malta. In all large and medium towns in the kingdoms, the Lodges exchanged "assurances of friendship," welcomed travelling Brothers, corresponded, and cultivated invisible but very real connections throughout Europe. Many young knights were therefore initiated during their period of training in Malta (their "caravans"). Once they returned to the continent, they practiced Masonry, thus contributing to the "Universal Republic of Freemasons," in the words of Pierre-Yves Beaurepaire.

I. Freemasonry in Malta

A/ The First Stones (1730–circa 1750)

Malta appears as one of the first territories in which modern Freemasonry established itself, after Great Britain, the Netherlands, and France. In fact, the first account of the existence of a Lodge on the island dates back to 1730. Shortly before February 14, 1730, the Bailiff of Brandenburg, Philip Guttenburg, made a donation to fund the building of a house for a Masonic Lodge in Msida.[3] Although few traces remain, this early Masonic presence did not escape contemporaries, because in

[1] We wish to thank the *Société de l'Histoire et du Patrimoine de l'Ordre de Malte* (History and Heritage Society of the Order of Malta) and the curator of its archives and its library, Mr. Hugues Lépolard. We are also grateful to our friend Jean-Claude Momal, who helped us with this research and with whom we are working on a prosopography of Freemason Knights of Malta in the eighteenth century, as an extension to this study. Finally, we have drawn significantly on Alain Blondy's excellent book, L'*Ordre de Malte au XVIIIe siècle, des dernières splendeurs à la ruine* (Paris: Bouchène, 2002).

[2] Pierre Mollier, Director of the Grand Orient de France Library and of the Museum of Freemasonry (Paris).

[3] Cited by A.J. Aegius, *History of Freemasonry in Malta 1730–1998* (Valletta: Stiges, 1999), 8. The author refers to the following serial number in the Archives of the Order of Saint John, kept in Malta's National Archives: AOM 1187, page 227.

1740, the inquisitor Ludovico Gualtieri asked Rome what position should be adopted regarding the Freemasons. He was reminded of the 1738 condemnation and invited to pressure the Grand Master of the Order (Raymond Despuig) to publish the *In Eminenti* bull… and to clamp down.[4] So the Grand Master then expels the (French) knights Livry,[5] as well as some of his friends for being Freemasons. Despuig died on January 15, 1741. A few months later his successor, Pinto, banished six other knights from the island for attending Masonic meetings.[6] Correspondence with Rome by the inquisitors Passionei (1743–1754) and then Salviati (1754–1759) shows that the religious authorities often dealt with cases of knights who were Freemason.[7] For example, on September 24, 1757, Cardinal Corsini told the inquisitor Salviati about his suspicions concerning the knights Capons, Somma, Pinto (probably a relative of the Grand Master Serviene), Vaccene, Abela, Grilert, Micallef, Morelli, and Wodworth.[8]

B/ The Lante Trial and the *Perfect Harmony* (1756–1776)

Over a period of around 20 years, there were many incidents demonstrating the presence of Freemasonry in Malta, particularly within the Order of Saint John of Jerusalem. Pushed by the inquisitor, against a background of traditional rivalry between the ecclesiastical authorities and those of the Order, the Grand Master regularly took measures against Freemasons (often the severe penalty of banishment). In April 1776, there was a move from condemnation in principle and ad-hoc measures against individuals to a true official investigation on Freemasonry in Malta, led by the inquisitor Antonio Lante. The investigations began in a charged context, five months after the election of Rohan and seven months after the "priests' revolt." Because of an awareness of the sensitive nature of the subject, the trial took place *in camera* (in relative secrecy). This meticulous police work yielded a highly interesting report[9] on the situation in the 1750s and 1760s. However, very soon, the investigation came to affect everyone, including the inquisitor himself, who was surprised to discover that three of his close circle were Lodge leaders! The ecclesiastical authorities, who had probably supported the initiative as part of their permanent attempts to limit the independence of the Order, learned that several canons of the Cathedral were Masons. As for Rohan, after just a few months in charge, he had

---

[4] AIM, Lettere della Suprema Congregazione, 27 (1739–1783), fº54: "In ordinea quanto Vostra Signoria ha esposto rispetto alla Società dei Liberi Muratori […] questa Supreme Sagra Congregazione non ha guidicato espediente di trasmetterle altro se non che diversi esemplari della Constitutione Pontifica, con cui la detta società fu gia proibita e condennata […] Proceda contra quelle persone che usassero tuttavia di fare simili adunanze o ascriversi alla mentovata compagnia," cited in Aegius, *History of Freemasonry in Malta*, 9.

[5] It seems there was a significant Masonic hub around Livry from the end of the 1730s. See: Pierre Chevallier, *Le Sceptre, la Crosse et l'Equerre sous Louis XV et Louis XVI 1725–1789* (Paris: Honoré Champion, 1996), 47.

[6] *Political State of Great Britain* LIX (1740): 427. Cited by Desmond Caywood, "Freemasonry and the Knight of Malta," *Ars Quatuor Coronatorum* 83 (1971): 72.

[7] See Aegius, *History of Freemasonry in Malta*, ISSN 10–11.

[8] AIM, Corr. 30, fº 309, cited in Aegius, *History of Freemasonry in Malta*, 11.

[9] See John Montalto, *The Nobles of Malta 1530–1800* (Malta: Midsea Books Ltd, 1979). John Montalto devotes a whole chapter (XIX-Freemasonry) to describing and analyzing this remarkable document. The serial number of the piece in the Malta Inquisition archives is A.I.M. Ms. Processo Lante.

the humiliation of seeing his name cited several times. Not only were there allusions to the Grand Master's Masonry (he was actually initiated to a Lodge in Parma in July 1756), but there were also persistent references to his relative, Prince Camille de Rohan, whose palace in La Valette was one of Malta's most active Masonic centers. The names of many knights, particularly French knights, were revealed. After a few weeks, the inquisition investigators realized they had underestimated the scale of the Masonic phenomenon on the island and in the Order... Finally, following a "regrettable" filing error, the report was "misplaced" and consequently not sent to the Inquisition headquarters in Rome. It was only found 30 years ago, in the Cathedral archives.

One of the main suspects questioned and whose statement is reported was the knight Formosa de Fremeaux. In his interrogation, he explains how he was initiated in 1756, by a Lodge working in Msida. A few days later, he visited another Lodge, led by the knight de Crusyol (Crussol?), who sat in Pawla. Immediately, Formosa de Fremeaux appeared as a highly zealous Mason. He admitted to having had Masonic symbols painted in his house in Zejtun and to hosting a Lodge in his La Valette residence to receive the knight Guasconi, who had come especially from Palermo to be initiated. He gives quite a detailed description of the Masonic ceremonies. From the details he presents, it is clear that the Maltese Masons practiced the Masonic Rite that was used in France at the time, today called the "French Rite." Moreover, the license of the third Lodge cited in the Lante report came from France. On February 13, 1766, in Tou-

lon, Brother Beufier de la Louerie gave the knight Lincel a warrant to create a Lodge in Malta, with the distinctive name of the *Perfect Harmony*. Lincel delegated his warrant to another knight, who would be an active Mason until the end of the century: Ligondès, colonel of the Maltese regiment then chamberlain to the Grand Master. A formerly unknown account confirms and completes the documentation on the Lante trial. It was found in the travel journals of a young German aristocrat: Karl von Zinzendorf.[10] His journal indicates that he was received as a Mason in Malta in March 1766. The Lodge had by then changed its distinctive name slightly, to become *Saint John of Scotland of Secrecy and Harmony*, daughter of Marseille's *Saint John of Scotland*. The name stuck. In his journal on Malta, he also names other members of the Lodge, who like himself were Knights of Malta: Ligondès, Crose-Lincel (the two signatories of the license) Tommasi, Loras, Litta, Guillet de Monthouxanf, and the Prince of Caramanico's younger Brother, the Count of Aquino who accompanied Cagliostro during his stays in Naples, Malta, and Sicily. Most of these names recur later on...

C/ Saint John's Lodge of Secrecy and Harmony (1788–1792)

After the Lante report, the other main source for the history of Freemasonry in Malta is the file sent to the Grand Lodge of England by a group of Masons, to place under its Obedience their newly recreated Lodge with the distinctive name *Saint John's Lodge of Secrecy and Harmony*. Once again, the documents describe the situation at the

---

[10] Christine Lebeau studied the Zinzendorf Brothers outside of the Masonic context, in her thesis entitled *Aristocrates et grands commis à la cour de Vienne (1748–1791). Le modèle français* (Paris: CNRS, 1996). Our thanks to Pierre-Yves Beaurepaire, who directed us to this reference discovered by Helmut Watzlawick during his work on the publication of Zinzendorf's travel journals.

time of writing (around 1790), but by citing various Masonic antecedents, they give a great deal of information about the two preceding decades. Moreover, these were internal Masonic documents, so are much more precise concerning the names and masonic careers of the Brothers. Overall, this correspondence with London confirms the picture we have painted so far. The Masons of Malta write that:

> *From the start of the century, our Masonic association under the distinctive name of Harmony and Secrecy embraced and professed all the degrees of symbolic Masonry. Afterwards, in around 1764, our Brothers reunited under the Doctrine of the Lodges of Saint John of Scotland by affiliation with that of Marseille; from then on we remained custodians of the instructions and symbolic rituals up to the three Scottish Degrees, to which those of Knight of the Orient and Knight of the Sun and the Rosy Cross were joined by moral analogy or some other inclination. We preserve these various instructions in their entirety, and, moreover, some of the members [...] are decorated with the High Degrees of foreign or French Masonry.*[11]

Thus, the Maltese Masons used a typical eighteenth-century French Masonic structure. After the traditional Degrees of Apprentice, Fellow, and Master, the Brothers used a series of those high grades that were the privileged channels of esotericism

and the chivalric imagination in the century of Enlightenment. These rituals were particularly fashionable in the Lodges of southern France, particularly in Toulon, or around *Saint John of Scotland* in Marseille. Thus, the Knight of the Sun uses an astonishing alchemical symbolism concerning the Rosy Cross, which appears as an attempt to restore primitive Christianity by emphasizing its "initiatory" dimension. The Maltese Brothers explain the circumstances leading them to revive a Lodge which had not met for several years:

> *We, the undersigned Master, Fellow, and Apprentice Brothers, some from the old Maltese Lodge known as Saint John's Lodge of Secrecy and Harmony, some from other Lodges and under various systems.*
>
> *Regretfully long separated from the whole association and from Masonic work, but wishing to be reintegrated into the ancient practice of a wise and holy rule whose foundations and character will never be erased from our memory, we have eagerly seized the opportunity of the visit from the Very Reverend Brother Count von Kolowrat, current chamberlain to H.M. the Emperor to resume our old practices under his leadership.*[12]

This letter is particularly interesting, because for the first time, it gives the full list of the members of a Maltese Lodge. This shows how deeply Masonry was present at the heart of the Order of Saint John

---

[11] Translated from: Library-Archives of the United Grand Lodge of England, File on Saint John's Lodge of Secrecy and Harmony, serial number 1136, item 20/D/6, f°2: "Lettre adressée par les Frères de Malte à la Grande Loge – des 'Moderns' – à Londres, le 24 avril 1792." The original letter from the Brothers of Malta to the Grand Lodge of the "moderns" in London on April 24, 1792, is in French.

[12] Translated from: Library-Archives of the United Grand Lodge of England, File on Saint John's Lodge of Secrecy and Harmony, serial number 1136, item 20/D/2. Letter of June 30, 1788.

of Jerusalem. The seven founders were all knights. The list features many known names who had meanwhile progressed within the Order, with three becoming Great Crosses: Abel de Loras, then a pillar of the *Langue d'Auvergne* and a member of Grand Master Rohan's close circle, the bailiff Tommasi, former page to Pinto who became Grand Master during the difficult period of the early nineteenth century, and Count de Litta. Kolowrat was Grand Prior of Bohemia and one of Rohan's key men for relations with central Europe. Many members of the Lodge were not just knights: they were dignitaries of the Order. Thirty years later, Formosa de Fremeaux was still on board, and was joined by Ligondès, who even became Venerable (president) in 1790. Because of the atmosphere of growing confusion at the start of the 1790s, the Lodge became a gathering point for Masons, with around 40 Brothers. Over two thirds were knights of Saint John of Jerusalem; the others were either priests or often important employees of the Order, such as Doublet, who was secretary to the Grand Master. Although he was a Mason, there is no proof that Rohan participated in the works of *Saint John's Lodge of Secrecy and Harmony*. It is even very probable that he abstained, because of his position. However, several clues indicate that he was relatively sympathetic or at least benevolently neutral towards the Lodge.[13] Although he warns against hasty conclusions, Alain Blondy notes that *"the vast majority of knights who in one way or another held very important roles under Rohan's princedom, belonged to Masonry."*[14]

II. The Knights of Malta: a European Masonic Network

A/ Masonry connects Malta to the European Capitals

Although Freemasonry saw a certain success on the island throughout the eighteenth century and in Saint John of Jerusalem, it was also a part of the link between Malta and the different power centers in Europe. The knights travelled extensively. When they were young, they left the land of their birth to complete their "caravans" and spend at least the required period in Malta. Following this, their career in the Order brought them back to the continent to take charge of a Commanderie in France, Italy, Spain, Austria, etc. However, they regularly returned to the island to defend their interests at headquarters and obtain a more important role or position. Not to mention the Order's diplomatic staff in the various Catholic courts and the knights employed for a period in the national navies either in the headquarters or the major ports. There were far more knights of Malta across Europe than there were on the island. The knights' cosmopolitanism, which even became a sort of literary type, inevitably met that of Freemasonry. In fact, by their very nature, the Lodges (particularly in the eighteenth century) were a place of contact and exchange of "commerce" in the old sense of the word. This vocation defined the first article of the founding text of modern Freemasonry, Anderson's *Constitutions* (1723): *"Masonry becomes the Center of the Union, and the Means of conciliating true Friendship among Persons*

---

[13] There are two types of evidence for this: the ill will with which he followed repeated orders from the Holy See and from the Inquisition to crack down on the Masons, and the shining careers of most Lodge members within the Order.

[14] Translated from Alain Blondy, *L'Ordre de Malte au XVIIIe siècle*, 274.

that must else have remain'd at a perpetual Distance." The Brothers (of Malta!) of the Chevalier des Grieux must have been familiar with this precept repeated by the follower of another cult (though his type of devotions was not all that foreign to many "men of the Religion"):[15] Casanova, who explains in his *Mémoires*:

> *Every young man who travels, who wants to know the wide world, who does not want to be inferior to another and excluded from the company of his equals in our times, must be initiated into what we call Freemasonry.*[16]

Infused with the contemporary idea of the unity of humanity and with their aspiration to the utopia of a universal Brotherhood, Enlightenment thinkers scrupulously made connections with Freemasons in other towns and countries. The itinerant lifestyle of the knight Brothers meant they were inevitably very sensitive to this concept.

There were continuous Masonic links between Malta and the major French ports of the Mediterranean: Toulon and Marseille. From 1760 to 1780, the knights of Ligondès, Le Boscage, Vintimille, Seillons, La Tour du Pin, Pontévès, and Chabriant carried out Masonic works between Toulon and Malta.[17] In the same period, the Lodges of Marseille, with *Saint John of Scotland* at the forefront, regularly had commanders from Malta within their ranks: La Durane de Piolin, Hana, Vincencini[18] Foresta, and Vilhena.[19] As for Torring, a young Apprentice of the Lodge, he was "in Malta." The most unusual case preserved in the annals is that of the Lodge of Narbonne, led by the Chefdebien d'Armissan family. The oldest son was initiated in Malta during his "caravans," and when he returned to Narbonne, he created a Lodge there with his Brothers (the baron, abbot and knights of Chefdebien). There were no less than 13 knights of Malta among the lodge's 48 members.[20] Chefdebien was a passionate Mason in contact with his cousin d'Aigrefeuille, who himself corresponded with those Brothers most informed about

---

[15] Jean Potocki, who knew Malta well, having been received as a knight there in 1778 and stayed there for some time, gave the following words to one of the heroes in his extraordinary novel The Manuscript Found in Saragossa: "I entered Malta before leaving childhood [...], so I could and still can have a claim to the first Dignities of the Order. However, since these are accessed only later in life, and I had nothing to do in the meantime, I followed the example of our first bailiffs, who perhaps should have set me a better one. In a word, I spent my time making love." Translated from the French in René Radrizzani, *Histoire du commandeur de Toralva* (Paris: Edition José Corti, 1990), 535. Our thanks to Pierre Lachkareff for pointing out this rich reference to us. On this image in literature, it is also useful to consult Claire Eliane Engel's writings on their place in the Abbé Prévost's novels. See *Les Chevaliers de Malte* (Paris: Les Presses contemporaines, 1972), 249–253.

[16] Translated from Charles Porset, "Casanova Franc-maçon," *Chroniques d'Histoire maçonnique* 49 (1998): 5.

[17] *Tableau général des Frères qui composent la R∴ Loge de St. Jean de la Marine, sous le titre distinctif de la Parfaite Harmonie, constituée à l'Orient de Toulon le 20 avril 1764, arrêté le 14 mars 5785 [1785].* ("List of the Brothers of the St. Jean de la Marine Lodge, under the distinctive title of the Perfect Harmony, formed in the Orient of Toulon on April 20, 1764, stopped on March 14, 5785 [1785].")

[18] Jacques Choisey, *La Respectable Loge de Saint Jean d'Ecosse, Mère Loge Ecossaise à l'Orient de Marseille, entre 1762 et 1787* (Brussels: Ed. Memo & Codec, 1986), 47 and 49.

[19] *Tableau des Frères qui composent la T.R. Loge Saint Jean d'Ecosse, à l'Orient de Marseille [...] 1784* ("List of the Brothers in the *Saint Jean d'Ecosse* Lodge, in the Orient of Marseille [...] 1784,") [printed], Lib. GODF AR 113-2, item 517.

[20] Rite Primitif, *Tableau de la première [loge] du Rite Primitif en France* (Narbonne, 1790).

the Mysteries of the (Masonic) Order in Paris, Lyon, and even Germany. Alain Blondy also describes the case of... *Saint John of Jerusalem*,[21] who from Saône to Rhône gathered several knights around the commander Tulle de Villefranche, to the extent that the Lyon Brothers simply called the group "the Malta Lodge."[22] On December 13, 1766, the young knight Karl von Zinzendorf, who we left as a Mason in Malta, was in Strasbourg. He was participating in the work of the *Candeur* Lodge, to which he was introduced by another knight of Saint John of Jerusalem, Brother Flachslanden, second warden of the lodge.[23] *La Candeur* was a real nerve-center for links with Germany and central Europe.[24]

When *Saint John's Lodge of Secrecy and Harmony* reformed in 1788, it showed great concern to establish solid relationships with England. The correspondence contains many expressions of allegiance to the Grand Lodge of London. The Brothers emphasize *"the Most Reverend Brother the Count von Kolowrat [... who made us] determined to resume our works under the regime of the Supreme Lodge of England."* He was the man in charge of presenting and defending the case before the English, with whom he seemed

to have privileged links.[25] However, Kolowrat was not only the guarantor of the London-Malta link. He also maintained strong relationships with other European Masonic centers. Thus, a few years before, he took part in an important event for French and German Masonries. It is surprising to find on the *"Table of deputies in the General Congress of Freemasons under the Rectified Rite gathered in Wilhelmsbad from July 16 to September 1, 1782 [...] the Count von Kolowrat Liebstein, Chamberlain to H.M. Imperial, in O. Fr. Franciscus Eq. Ab Aquila fulgente, with the full powers of the Chapter of Saint Hypolite in Vienna and of Hermandstadt in Transylvania."*[26] Introduced into the Grand Lodge of England, Brother Kollowrat was also a familiar of Germanic Masonry. However, the international contacts of the Maltese Lodge also extended to other areas. At a time when the Brothers were trying to establish themselves under English protection, some of the most eminent members of the Lodge being composed also belonged to another Lodge in Rome, this time under the Paris Obedience. In fact, a record of the *Réunion des Amis Intimes* is to be found in the archives of the Grand Orient de France,[27]

---

[21] From the first half of the eighteenth century, it was common to see a rapprochement between Freemasonry and the knightly orders, and many Lodges used the name *Saint John of Jerusalem*. The Lodge created in Nancy in 1772 still exists today, under the Obedience of the Grand Orient de France.

[22] Alain Blondy, L'Ordre de Malte au XVIIIe siècle, 267.

[23] Strasbourg National University Library, Manuscript 5437, *Registre des procès-verbaux de la loge de la Candeur constituée mère des loges du Grand Orient de Strasbourg*, f° 176. Our thanks to Pierre-Yves Beaurepaire for bringing this reference to our attention.

[24] Pierre-Yves Beaurepaire, *L'autre et le Frère, l'étranger et la Franc-maçonnerie en France au XVIIIe siècle France* (Paris: Honoré Champion, 1998), particularly chapter 9: "La Candeur, orient de Strasbourg: un creuset maçonnique," 399–443. At the start of the 1770s, there was another Maltese knight in the ranks: de Brülh.

[25] In fact, the register of the Grand Secretary of London includes several letters exchanged with Kolowrat, particularly on the affairs of Naples where Masonry had been banned. These show a mutual understanding between the two correspondents. See Alain Blondy, *L'Ordre de Malte au XVIIIe siècle*, 76.

[26] Grand Prieuré des Gaules, Les Cahiers verts, *Les Convents du Régime Ecossais Rectifié*, special edition (Paris, 2005), 144–146.

[27] The Grand Orient de France's correspondence archives for this period are currently kept in the *Cabinet des manuscrits*. BnF, FM2 575.

for which the Venerable in 1789 was... the bailiff Abel de Loras. Its members included Count von Kolowrat and the knight Guillet de Monthoux, Loras's nephew and adoptive son.

This situation illustrates both the mobility of Malta's high executives within Enlightenment Europe and the way in which the new Masonic network was coupled with and completed the old Maltese network. In the late 1780s, the (main?) Lodge of Malta, which seems to have been a sort of annex of a part of the Order's leadership, was consequently in contact with the Masonic centers of London, Paris, and Rome, with a few connections in Germany and Austria. Again, over-interpretation should be avoided. However, it is necessary to note that in Malta, Loras and Kolowrat were the leaders of the party wishing to free the Order from the direct and predominant influence of Versailles. The Grand Master had even stopped making decisions of any importance without the approval of the French Ministry. The enemies of the "French party" wanted to give the Order back some room for maneuver by rebalancing the powers that influenced it, particularly by trying to preserve relationships with the Court of Naples, with Spain in the background, and by bringing new players like Russia or England onto the Mediterranean scene. Thus, it is highly likely that the attachment of the *Secrecy and Harmony* to London, on Kolowrat's initiative, was not purely driven by Masonic motives. However, the affair would end badly. Loras[28] was in Rome in 1789, responsible for representing the Order to the Pope. He wanted to be made an official ambassador for Malta. Obviously, being both a representative of the Sovereign Order of Saint John of Jerusalem to the Holy See and a Worshipful Master chairing over a Lodge of the Grand Orient could pose problems for fault-finders.[29] However, his links with Cagliostro also worked against him. High on the list of the Inquisition's investigation of the "Grand Copht" of "Egyptian Masonry," he was forced to flee by night to Naples, where he took refuge. He then moved on to Malta, where (with mixed success) he tried to return to grace with the Grand Master Rohan.

B/ Three Good Reasons for Knights to be Masons

The cosmopolitanism to which knights were in some ways predisposed was one of the factors explaining their relative enthusiasm for Freemasonry, but it was not the only reason. There was also the spirit of the times, and Alain Blondy rightly emphasizes that it was in no way unusual for a knight of Malta in the eighteenth century to be a Mason. Knights were simply like the young, well-off people of any period, who had the leisure to take an interest in the innovations of their time. They could not remain unaware of the papal condemnation, but it is clear that few of them were frightened by it. Speaking to his ambassador in Rome, Cardinal Fleury answered without illusion that: "*The bull that the Pope has issued against the Freemasons may not be enough to abolish this Brotherhood, if there is no penalty besides the*

---

[28] Loras has a bad reputation and historians are often very critical about him. Without wishing to plead in his defense, two points explaining this severity can be discussed. Firstly, he was one of the main players of the party which was in fact hostile to France, which obviously wins him no favor from a primarily French historiography. Secondly, most of the accounts about his personality are from his sworn enemy (who was nevertheless a Brother in knighthood and Masonry), Dolomieu.

[29] The person finally named as ambassador, Camille de Rohan, also occupied these two positions.

fear of excommunication. The court of Rome applies this penalty so often that today, it has little preventive power."[30]

Aside from the spirit of the times (Marie-Antoinette wrote to her sister that "*everyone is a Freemason*"[31]) there are two more unexpected factors that explain the Masonic commitment of the knights of Malta. The first also concerns the mentality of the time, although in another register. Certain high-society Lodges were simply centers for noble sociability in the eighteenth century. Thus, the *Société Olympique* emanating from the *Olympique de la Parfaite Estime* Lodge contained 9 princes, 13 dukes, 55 marquises, 57 counts, 19 viscounts, and 13 barons... including 17 Knights of Malta, one of whom was the great Suffren. The *Candeur* Lodge (closely linked to Orléans) and the *Contrat Social* Lodge also contained many Maltese Masons. Similar situations were seen in the provinces although to a lesser extent. For example, in Toulouse, although there were several Knights of Malta in the ranks of the *Vérité Reconnue* Lodge, this was primarily because it was a meeting point for the local aristocracy. In fact, it was "*by far the most exclusive Lodge in the town, because it contained not only magistrates, military personnel, and gentlemen, but also no commoners, and because there were clearly more nobles of the sword than nobles of the robe.*"[32]

A third and final, more subtle and even more mysterious motive further explains the presence of knights in Lodges: some showed a clear interest in Christian esotericism. We will not retrace the relations between Loras and Cagliostro here. However, it is also unusual to observe the relative over-representation of the Maltese in Lodges professing the Rectified Scottish Rite: Chefdebien in Narbonne, Aigrefeuille in Montpellier then in Paris, du Bourg and Guibert in Toulouse, La Croix de Sayve in Grenoble, Monspey in Lyon... As for Kolowrat, he participated, but Chefdebien was also there at the founding event of the Rite: the Congress of Wilhelmsbad. Yet the Rectified Scottish Rite and its Order of Benevolent Knights of the Holy City saw themselves as restoring true chivalry in service of the most essential mysteries of Christianity. Its structures were those of an Order of chivalry. Its ceremonies and its instructions were meant to explain the relationships between God, men, and the universe by the mediation of Jesus Christ and intermediary spirits. The Knights of Malta therefore practiced a very distinctive type of Masonry.

The work of the Congress of Wilhelmsbad provides an interesting account of the esoteric speculations of certain Knights of Malta at debates concerning whether the Templars held occult knowledge. Brother Willermoz made a parallel with the Order of Malta and evoked the case of knights versed in these issues. The issue discussed was the presence, in the very structure of the Order of the Temple, of elements linked to the numerical symbolism that is so important in Freemasonry in general, and in the professed gnosis of theosophist Masons in particular:

---

[30] Translated from Pierre Chevallier, *Le Sceptre, la Crosse et l'Equerre sous Louis XV et Louis XVI 1725–1789* (Paris: Honoré Champion, 1996), 76.

[31] Translation of Pierre Chevallier's citation in: *Histoire de la Franc-maçonnerie française* (Paris: Fayard, 1974), t.I, 209. Source: Paul Vogt d'Hunolstein, *Correspondance inédite de Marie-Antoinette* (Paris: Dentu, 1864).

[32] Translated from Michel Taillefer, *La Franc-maçonnerie Toulousaine: 1741–1799* (Paris: Commission d'Histoire de la Révolution Française/ENSB-CTHS, 1984), 133.

We can observe that at the time of its greatest splendor, it was divided into nine Provinces, each governed by a Provincial Leader, that the number of nine leaders corresponds to the number of founders, coming to ten with its General Grand Master. Some state that this number expresses great things: this observation, which is rather indifferent to me, might be scorned and mocked by some, and perhaps it will also retain the attention of others. As for me, I leave it to each individual according to the meaning they wish to give it, noting only that when we want to verify the origin and goal of an Order or Society, we must not neglect any of the keys that might help with this verification. I further observe that the Order of Malta, born in the same place in almost the same period, appears to have been established on the same basis that it still retains today, although some tongues of this Order have ceased their action. Even today, it is represented in Malta by nine pillars or Order leaders under different names, who with their Grand Master make ten, and, in the General Chapters, by 27 representatives, who with the same Grand Master make 28, which comes down to the same; this conformity is interesting, and perhaps we might manage to find some even more interesting causes for it in the old archives of the Order. I know several of its members who are convinced of this. [33]

These interesting words were spoken at a small gathering before at least two other Knights of Malta: the Brothers (in Masonry) *Eques a Capite Galeato* (Chefdebien) and *ab Aquila Fulgente* (Kolowrat). Silence equals consent! The Maltese were perhaps also looking for an ideal (fantasy) chivalry in the High Degrees of Masonry: one which they could not find in the everyday life of the Order.[33]

Whatever the private reasons (social or "esoteric") which brought them to the Lodge, the knights subsequently practiced Masonry across Europe. Whether their works were in the spirit of Diderot's Encyclopedia or whether they heralded a romantic quest, for the Knights of Malta, membership of a Lodge was above all a way of being in their century, a means of connection to the present of their time. However, by partaking in this new sociability, which was the more or less legitimate offspring of Enlightenment thinkers, they in fact participated in a great change in minds and in a revolution "which everything seemed to portend, yet which nobody saw coming,"[35] according to the pertinent observation of Brother de Ségur.

It is necessary to avoid any anachronism. Although many eighteenth-century Lodges were sensitive to new ideas, they cannot under any circumstances be considered as a whole to have been a militant wing of the *philosophical party*. The fact that many Knights of Malta were Masons should not be interpreted as a conversion of Voltaire's and

---

[33] Translated from: Grand Prieuré des Gaules, Les Cahiers verts, "Préavis du Fr. ab Eremo, Gr. Grand Prieuré des Gaules, Les Cahiers verts,Chancelier de la IIe [province …] sur la question concernant la légitimité de la filiation de l'O. du T. avec notre système actuel […]," *Les Convents du Régime Ecossais Rectifié*, special edition, 53–54.

[34] Pierre Mollier, *La Chevalerie maçonnique: imaginaire chevaleresque, légende templière et Franc-maçonnerie au siècle des Lumières* (Paris: Dervy, 2005).

[35] *Mémoires du Comte de Ségur*, Tome II, 95. The Count of Ségur was not Maltese, but he left an excellent description of his reception into the *Ordre de Saint Lazare*, comparing this venerable ceremony and the evolution of the century.

Diderot's ideas. One current of Masonry, well-represented in Malta, arises more from a pre-romantic sensibility, or even from what could be called the "anti-Enlightenment thinkers." Masonic initiation was in this case probably experienced as a way of reconnecting with the true knightly essence of the Order. From the 1790s, the strong presence of Masonry at the highest level of Saint John of Jerusalem provoked comments about a "Masonic conspiracy" which supposedly influenced the leaders of the Order and finally led to the fall of Malta. This theory attributes to it a unity of thought and action that it never possessed and still does not possess. Thus, two of the most significant Mason-Knights, Loras and Dolomieu, fought so bitterly that if Masonry did in a way weaken the Order, it was more by internal disputes than by any mythical conspiracy! However, the Maltese Lodge, with its branches in the main European capitals, brought together knights who defended fairly similar positions within Saint John of Jerusalem. Consequently, it seems that Masonry did constitute a sort of "party" with Loras and Kolowrat as its figureheads. This party had a following in de Rohan's Princedom and attempted to play a part after 1797. For a while, in fact, *the bailiff de Loras, having subjugated the Grand Master, controlled [...] the policy of Malta.*[36] Thus the "Lodge of the knights" probably had an influence, but its real nature and extent are difficult to judge in the power balances among which Malta tried to defend its position in the Mediterranean setting.

---

[36] Translated from Alain Blondy, L'*Ordre de Malte au XVIIIe siècle*, 258–259.

Freemasonry and the Risk of Geopolitics in the Eighteenth Century

Yves Hilvert-Messeca[1]

If we base our judgment on Alexandre Defay's statement that "geopolitics studies interactions between the geographical space and the resulting power conflicts," it is arguable that from its very beginnings as an institution and an ideology, Masonry had a geopolitical dimension.

It is the vocation of every Mason, every Lodge, and every Masonic body to convert others, develop, survive, and therefore occupy and "exploit" a real and/or imaginary territory. Throughout the eighteenth century, Brothers, Lodges, and/or Obediences created networks that formed the Masonic ecumene. The geopolitical boom of Freemasonries was to reveal a certain mobility—practices of travel, hospitality, and epistolary and economic exchange. Travel was common practice in the Enlightenment. It was not a new habit, but it had become an illustration of man's quest to explore the world and its phenomena, and expand his knowledge.

Masons traveled the world as they traveled between Lodges. The art of travel thus favored and worked through Masonic networks. Travel made it possible to recognize and claim territories and spaces. A Masonic geopolitics of travel developed, based around networks of communication and affinities between Brothers, around those of Masonic organizations claiming transnational status (Cosmopolitan Lodges, Mother Lodges, and Obediences) that wanted to organize space according to a particular Masonic logic and design, or around those of states hoping to territorialize their Masonry and bring it under state control, while using it to serve their geopolitical and geoeconomic ambitions. The main social players in this geopolitics were travelers and migrants, princes, aristocrats, sons from rich families on the Grand Tour, diplomats, soldiers, sailors, men of religion, merchants, paleotourists, French pastors, exiled British Jacobites, artists, actors, tutors, students, and adventurers like Cagliostro (1743–1795) or Giovanni-Jacopo Casanova (1725–1798). Throughout the century, a veritable *universal republic of Freemasons*, a Masonic world and its corpus, was built. This republic was neither a contingent liberal and/or democratic political form, nor a state. Rather, it transcended and was widespread in both of these. It constituted a geopolitical project. This project was original and universal in terms of its geographical extent (even if it was in fact centered around the Atlantic, the North Sea, the Baltic, and the northern shores of the Mediterranean), its sociocultural composition of theoretically equal brothers of diverse religions (even if very few came from the *Respublica cristiana*) and opinions, its unusual structure's combining of the Ancien Regime and modernity, and its common goal's focus on several principles that were not always followed, namely the sincere practice of virtue, the disinterested acquisition of knowledge, and the unremitting search for the truth.

---

[1] Yves Hilvert-Messeca, Groupe Société-Religion-Laïcité (CNRS).

[2] Alexandre Defay, *La Géopolitique* (Paris: PUF, 2004), 4.

Masonic geopolitics also relied on correspondence. Masons, Lodges, and Obediences progressively built up an official corpus that was laid down with paper and ink. Tellingly, "being in the correspondence of" meant belonging to the network of a Lodge or Hiramic organization. There was a flow of official and/or private correspondence between Brothers, Lodges, and Masonic institutions, aiming to establish the legitimacy, prestige, and authority of the author, or even the receiver. Before long, power issues developed around correspondence networks, which became a source of endless rivalries, quarrels, and disputes. Throughout the century, patents became the focal point for Masonic geopolitics. The distribution of patents by Masons, Lodges, or Obediences to other Masons, Lodges, or Obediences for the purposes of Lodge formation, making Masons, awarding Degrees, or practicing rites became an important issue. He who solicited it sought legitimacy for his foundation, and he who transmitted it hoped to strengthen his network. Because sthere was no such thing as being too careful, patents were sought readily. Thus the *Candeur* Lodge, based in Strasbourg, sought patents from the first Grande Loge de France (GLDF; Grand Lodge of France) in 1763, then from the Grande Loge des Modernes (Grand Lodge of the Moderns) in 1772, of which it became number 429. It also sought inclusion in the *Directoire Ecossais de Bourgogne* (Scottish Directory of Burgundy), and aggregation letters from the Grand Orient de France (GODF; Grand Orient of France) in 1777. Patents became an object of pride and an instrument of control, or even a source of revenue.

However, Masons in the eighteenth century were both citizens of the afore-mentioned "republic" and citizens of a real country, which implied certain geographical constraints. The toing and froing of the Bordeaux Anglaise (English), which was founded in 1732 by Irish sailors and merchants but broadened its recruitment to French natives and adopted French as its liturgical language, was typical. The organization received new constitutions from the Grande Loge des Modernes in March 1766, and successively bore the numbers 363 (1766), 298 (1770), 240 (1781), and 204 (1792) of this Obedience, while itself forming other Lodges such as *La Française*, headquartered in Bordeaux (1740). Entering into the correspondence of the GODF, it received letters of aggregation from it in 1780. After itself setting up another organization in Bordeaux, the *Etoile Flamboyante aux Trois Lys* (Blazing Star of the Three Lilies), it was ostracized by the GODF, which confirmed the revocation of its correspondence in 1785. A minority of its members founded the *Vraie Loge Anglaise* (True English Lodge), patented by Paris in the same year. In 1790, the *Anglaise* sought new letters of aggregation from the GODF, but these were refused. The affair was not resolved until 1803.

Thus, Freemasonry was both a product and a producer of geopolitics, but in turn, it could itself become intertwined with the geopolitical undertakings of others. Throughout the whole century, it would interfere, interdepend, or compete with academies, salons, clubs, religious brotherhoods, cafés, and inns. There was consequently a geopolitics of what Daniel Roche calls "the Enlightenment space."[3] Sometimes, Freemasonry would be instrumentalized by other structures, particularly certain groups and states attempting to use

---

[3] Daniel Roche, *Le Siècle des Lumières en province. Académies et académiciens provinciaux 1680–1789* (Paris: Mouton, 1978), 1:300.

it for their own geopolitical ends. This explains the presence of "communitarian-national" Lodges in the Kingdom of Naples or the Ottoman Empire. Similarly, in Russia in the 1770s and 1780s, the three thousand Masons and hundred or more Lodges were divided. Some followed the English influence behind the poet Ivan P. Elaguine (1726–1793), secretary to Catherine II, named by London, and provincial Grand Master in 1772. Others joined the action of the Swedish System led by Prince Alexander B. Kurakin (1752–1818), and Prince Gavrii P. Gagarin (1745–1808). Meanwhile, some moved toward the Strict Templar Observance,[4] with Count A. I. Musin-Puskhin (1744–1811) and General Piotr I. Mélissino, of Greek origin (1726–1797). Others were Prussophilic, with the Zinnendorf Rite introduced by Baron Johann von Reichel (1729–1791). Geopolitical ambitions and strategies encapsulated Masonic objectives, with brothers easily moving between Obediences according to their interests and/or choices. These switches also showed the grasp that autocratic power had over the Russian Lodges and their adaptation to the foreign policy of Saint Petersburg. At a time when benevolence, happiness, urbanity, and virtue were meant to come together, Masons, Lodges, and Obediences mostly occupied the openings in Ancien Regime society. However, they did not break with it. They forged out microspaces of meeting and expression, simultaneously borrowing from ancient or supposedly ancient configurations, riding the associative structures of modernity, and benefiting as much as possible from the opportunities of the time. Thus, progressively and increasingly, a Masonic geopolitics grew up. Its success varied between climates and over the years.

Individual Masons played a part in this development, for example the German, Stürtz, whom Pierre-Yves Beaurepaire charmingly called a "traveling salesman for the Royal Art."[5] With patents from the Berlin Union Lodge, in the 1740s he formed Lodges and initiated dozens of Brothers, particularly in Frankfurt am Main, in addition to the postmagistral degrees that he distributed freely. Certain elitist Lodges also entered into a geopolitical construction, for example the *Anglaise* (Bordeaux), the *Vrais Amis de l'Union* (True Friends of the Union) of Brussels, the *Pera Oriental* (Constantinople), the *Union* (Frankfurt), the *Irlandaise du Soleil Levant* (Irish Lodge of the Rising Sun, Paris), which received medical students from Eire, the *Candeur* (Strasburg), and The Crowned Hope (Vienna). An archetypal example was *Saint Jean d'Ecosse* (Saint John of Scotland), based in Marseille, which on the brink of the Revolution became a veritable Obedience with around 30 affiliated Lodges in the French Mediterranean Midi, on the maritime routes of the Levant (Eastern Mediterranean), and in the Antilles, as well as contacts with around a hundred groups throughout Europe. Three-quarters of the members of *Saint-Jean d'Ecosse* were merchants or similar. The great endogamous families of the Marseilles Chamber of Commerce (Audibert, Clary, Hughes, Isnard, Samatan, Seymandi, Tarteiron) were dominant. For the overrepresented Protestant elites, it provided social recognition and a means of integration. Its members also included most consuls installed in the port (Austria, Denmark, Piedmont-Sardinia, Poland, and Tuscany), as well as eminent representatives of the local nobility and the

---

[4] See below.

[4] Pierre-Yves Beaurepaire, *L'Espace des francs-maçons. Une sociabilité européenne au XVIIIe siècle* (Rennes: Presses Universitaires de Rennes, 2003), 99-102.

royal authorities. The organization had a true geopolitical strategy. Affiliation with the network was free: a weighty argument compared to the "free donation" (taxes) required by the GODF. The Daughter Lodges (Genoa, Palermo, Valletta, Salonika, and Constantinople) positioned themselves on the commercial routes of the port city. In Smyrna (which had 100,000 inhabitants at the time, half of whom were Muslims and a third of whom were Greek), the Marseille branch bore an almost programmatic name: *Saint-Jean d'Ecosse* des Nations Réunies (Saint John of Scotland of the Reunited Nations). It was a meeting place for Western merchants and a few representatives of the local economic elites (almost exclusively Christians). However, like most Lodges at the time, it practiced a flexible form of Masonry as a result of structural weaknesses (high absenteeism, turnover, selective and variable charitable activities, individual conflicts for power, and so forth) that often depended on the geopolitical context.

However, it is on the level of Obediences that a geopolitical analysis is most relevant. In theory, the Masonic cosmos extended worldwide. In reality, it equated to the European world. Several Obediential conceptions competed to structure it. Broadly, four are most noteworthy:

a) The English conception. Very early on, the Grand Lodge of London (later the Grand Lodge of the Moderns) theorized the constitution of a sort of Masonic Commonwealth organized around itself: the self-proclaimed Mother Lodge of the World. It had a sort of unbalanced condominium (London dominating) with the Grand Lodges of Ireland and Scotland, and a constitution policy outside England of provincial Grand Lodges and 30 provincial Grand Masters, named from 1730 to

1789. Some were without a group, and some pursued independence, such as François Bonaventure du Mont, Marquis of Gages (1739–1787), who was made provincial Grand Master of the Austrian Netherlands (now Belgium) in 1770. He made his province an autonomous Masonic entity, neglecting to pay taxes to London and delivering patents. In theory, the English Obedience did not give itself the power to directly create Lodges in the geopolitical sphere of the provincial Grand Lodges. However, it often betrayed this principle. Above all, the Grand Lodge of the Moderns gave itself the proclaimed right to recognize (or not) a Masonic body and proclaim it regular (or irregular), whilst opposing the territorialization and nationalization of Masonic organizations. However, the main reason for the failure of this geopolitical model was the long war (1751–1813) between the Moderns and the Ancients in England and in the British colonies, and the resistance of the national and nationalist Obediences to London.

b) The "Germanic" conception, represented by the Strict Templar Observance, was formed in the 1750s by the Silesian Baron Carl Gotthelf von Hund und Altengrotkau (1722–1776). It would collapse due to its Germano-centricism (among other things) after the death of Duke Ferdinand of Brunswick-Luneburg-Wolfenbuttel (1721–1792), who became its last Grand Master in 1772. The Strict Templar Observance was a part of the constant activity of the trans-German secret societies that participated in the political and cultural homogenization process affecting the German-speaking elites. It can therefore be seen as the Masonizing version of the *Reichspub-*

lizistik, the vast corpus of juridical and historical texts gathered in the seventeenth and eighteenth centuries, giving rise to a public space of discussion on the nature of the Reich. This "Germanic corps" sought both a geopolitical reality and a *corpus mysticum*. In a way, the Strict Templar Observance presented itself as a contribution by "Germanic" Masons to a project of basing a dream of a Masonic Reich on real geopolitical foundations. One might venture to say that it was, in a way, a sort of Masonic holy universal empire with a German aristocratic base. In a religiously divided Europe, this project sought to reunite the continent around a "primitive" ecumenical Christianity, or around a (Catholic sensu stricto) universal religion. Consequently, it is no surprise that, in this geopolitical vision of a European world reunified via a chivalric Freemasonry, the Romanian Prince Alexander Murusi, hospodar of Wallachia, envisaged projects for military drafting in order to reconquer the earthly Jerusalem. However, as was often the case, conflict got in the way. Various Masons like Joseph de Maistre (1753–1821) or Jean-Baptiste Willermoz (1730–1824) wanted to use the Strict Templar Observance to bring back the lost sheep of Protestantism, or even of the Orthodoxy, into the bosom of the Holy Roman Church, contributing to the global failure.

c) The French conception. As soon as it liberated itself from London, the first Grande Loge de France (GDLF) (1736–1776) developed a relative geopolitical strategy. It attempted, in vain, first to control all the Masons and organizations in the kingdom. In 1765, it set up a commission in charge of orga-nizing the Masonic corps on national lines. The treaty signed that year with the Grande Loge des Modernes was only a sort of ephemeral gentleman's agreement. Paris would ask all Lodges in France, established by London, to be reconstituted by Paris. This was not without its problems, as shown for example by the reservations of the *Anglaise*, based in Bordeaux. However, London would have liked to treat the first GLDF like a simple provincial Grand Lodge. The successor to the GLDF, the Grand Orient de France (GODF), founded in 1773, attempted to impose a heliocentric Masonic geopolitical project: a series of national Obediences "orbiting" the GODF, the new sun of the Hiramic world. The 1775–1777 attempts to reach a new treaty with London failed, particularly because they took place in the context of the War of Independence with the future United States (1775–1783). After the decline of the Strict Templar Observance in German-speaking lands, the influence of the GODF became dominant in continental Europe, particularly in Denmark, the Rhino-Westphalian regions, the Austrian Netherlands, and various ports in Italy or Poland. As was the case for London, outside of the French frontiers, the resistance of certain national Obediences would break the Masonic heliocentrism of the GODF. In France, the GODF's inability to unify French Freemasonry and create a single system of postmagistral degrees, particularly its rivalry with the Grand Orient dit de Clermont (1773–1799), as well as the resistance of various Mother Lodges like the Marseille Lodge Saint-Jean d'Ecosse, would impede the French Masonic geopolitics.

d) The Prussian–Swedish conception, or Freemasonry as an ideological tool of the state. In various states, Freemasonry was more or less integrated in an authoritarian way into the state system. This was the case for Prussia. King Friedrich II protected the Berlin Lodge *Zu den Drei Weltkugen* (Three Globes), which was founded in 1740 and became, on June 24, 1744, the Grosse Konïgliche-Mutterloge. In 1774, he gave "his very gracious protection, safeguard, and favor"[6] to the young Grosse Landesloge der Freimaurer von Deutschland in Berlin, founded in 1770 on the initiative of Johann Zinnendorf (1731–1782). A few weeks before his death, the monarch guaranteed, in a letter addressed to the *Royal York zur Freundschaft*,[7] that any virtuous Mason and good citizen could count on his protection. His nephew and successor, Friedrich Wilhelm II, king in 1786, protector of the Three Globes Mother Lodge (1770) and honorary member of the Berlin Lodge Three Golden Keys (1772), stopped frequenting Lodges, but on February 9, 1976, he confirmed his protection to the Order. In a letter of December 29, 1797, to the Grand Lodge Royal York, his son Friedrich Wilhelm III, King (though profane) of Prussia in 1797, cleared the Prussian Masons of suspicions of "subversive undertakings."[8] A few days later, he gave this Obedi-

ence the rights already enjoyed by the two other Grand Lodges. In an edict of October 20, 1798, the king banned illicit meetings and secret societies, but Article III made an exception for the three Obediences given exclusive practice[9] of Freemasonry in Prussia. The three institutions became a sort of entrusted Masonic public service. In exchange for a protective state monopoly, they became state instruments. In Sweden, King Adolf I Frederick became protector and *Obergrofmeister* of Swedish Freemasonry in 1753. Upon his accession, his son, Gustav III, king from 1771 to 1792, was proclaimed protector of the Order, then *Vicarius Salomonis*. His brother Charles, Duke of Södermanland and future Charles XIII, became *Orden Meister* and Grand Master of Freemasonry. He unified Freemasonry and set up a new Masonic, esoteric-Christian regime called the Swedish System, organized into three classes and eight degrees. In order to fully integrate it into power, in 1811, Charles XIII established a state decoration, the Order of Charles XIII, limited to 30 members, who had to be Masons. It still exists today. The Swedish System became monopolistic in Sweden, but expanded with the geopolitical developments of the Kingdom of Sweden. Around the Baltic, between competition and cooperation, state Freemasonries of riparian states

---

[6] Translator's note: Quotation back-translated from the French-language version of this article.

[7] Coming out of a Berlin Lodge of the Three Globes Mother Lodge, the Three Doves Lodge, created by Frenchmen in May 1760, became the Friendship of the Three Doves in 1761, and then the Royal York of Friendship after Prince Edward, duke of York and brother of King George III was admitted. In June 1789, the Lodge split off and proclaimed itself the Grosse Loge von Prussen (Grand Lodge of Prussia), then in 1845 it added Gennant Royal York zur Freunschaft (Called Royal York of Friendship) to its distinctive name.

[8] Translator's note: Quotation back-translated from the French-language version of this article.

[9] The monopoly was only ended in 1893 by a ruling from the High Administrative Court of Berlin.

served to support their geopolitics, and acted as an ideological instrument within state boundaries.

Overall, Masonic geopolitics overlapped with the political interests and economic interests of states. In the course of the century, the Order became diluted, despite the vain attempts of international convents to define Masonic "science." These included Altenberg (1745), Kolho (1772), Brunswick (1775), Lyon (1778), Wolfenbüttel (1778), Wilhelmsbad (1782), and those of the Philalethes (1784/5 and 1787). Ultimately, the Order wanted to construct the new Temple of Jerusalem, there and then. It is also important to consider Masonic geopolitical utopias such as the project of Baron von Hund (mentioned above), who wanted to make Labrador a model colony populated with nobles and sheltered from the passions and vices of the profane world, or the "nesomanic" projects for ideal Hiramic cities in Australia or Lampedusa. Alas, the Brothers, Lodges, and Obediences often wallowed in a profane new Babel. No transnational Masonic system succeeded in imposing itself. Despite the dream of ecumenism, universalist discourses, and ambient cosmopolitanism, the increasingly polymorphous Freemasonry of the eighteenth century gradually became nationalized.

Selected Bibliography:

Beaurepaire, Pierre-Yves. *La République Universelle des francs-maçons. De Newton à Metternich*. Rennes: Ouest-France, 1999.

Beaurepaire, Pierre-Yves. *L'Europe des francs-maçons*. Paris: Belin, 2002.

Beaurepaire, Pierre-Yves. *L'Espace des francs-maçons. Une sociabilité européenne au XVIIIe*. Rennes: Presses Universitaires de Rennes, 2003.

Giarrizzo, Giuseppe. *Massoneria e Illuminismo nell'Europa del Settecento*. Venice, Italy: Marsiglio, 1992.

Hivert-Messeca Yves, *L'Europe sous l'acacia, Vol. 1. Le XVIIIe siècle*. Paris: Dervy, 2012.

Jacob, Margaret. *Living Enlightenment: Freemasonry and Politics in Eighteenth Century Europe*. Oxford: Oxford University Press, 1991.

Reinalter, Helmut. *Die Rolle der Freimaurerei und Geheimgesellschaften im 18. Jahrhundert*. Innsbruck, Austria: Scientia 39, 1995.

Mormon Temple Rituals, Women and Freemasonry[1]

Carter Charles[2]

The Church of Jesus Christ of Latter-day Saints—or "Mormon Church" as it is commonly referred to—was organized in April 1830 and is rooted in the highly charged evangelical context of the Second Great which swept the East of the USA. Aside from its tag-carrying missionaries, it can readily be identified by its temples.[3] They differ in many ways from its smaller, and rather ordinary, "meeting houses" or "churches" used for Sunday services and cultural activities. Unlike the former, its temples are easily identifiable edifices topped by a golden angel—named Moroni—who is sounding a trumpet. Its meeting houses are open to members and non-members alike, whatever the ritual performed therein. On the other hand, once the temples are "dedicated to the Most High," only members who meet certain strict requirements are allowed to enter them and participate in a variety of soteriological rituals.

The architectural decorations and inscriptions on some of the Mormon Church's temples testify to a deep Masonic heritage. Indeed, the Mormon Church once openly proclaimed its Masonic identity, inherited from a time when it did not bode well to be a Mason in the USA. **This is** is why it now takes little effort on the part of one versed in Masonry to recognize Masonic elements in a Mormon ritualized handshake or to identify on the façade of the Church's temple in Salt Lake City the Eye of Providence in a circle that represents the Sun.[4] And the Church's leaders once displayed – literally "on the house top" – this Masonic heritage on a temple they erected in Nauvoo, Illinois, in 1846. The crowning element of that temple was a very particular weathervane made of a square and a compass and, just below it, was an angel with a special cap flying in the horizon while sounding a trumpet and carrying a book.[5] As shall be shown fur-ther, this public recognition of the Masonic aspects in Mormonism and the Church's

---

[1] This paper is an expanded version of "Mormonisme et franc-maçonnerie : du rôle des femmes dans les rituels du temple mormon" (Charles 2011, 281-297) in *Les femmes et la franc-maçonnerie. Des lumières à nos jours*, eds. Cécile Révauger and Jacques Lemaire. Belgium: La Pensée et les Hommes, 2011.

[2] Carter Charles, University Bordeaux-Montaigne, France.

[3] The Mormon Church has 141 temples in operation around the world, the majority of them being in North America.

[4] For Mormons like Greg Kearny, who is also a Mason like his father, the Masonic elements in Mormonism can be explained by the fact that its founding prophet saw Freemasonry as a vehicle, a "remarkable power of ritual form as a means of teaching complex ideas" (Kearny 2005).

[5] For an official source, see the scanned-copy published by the Church on the following Internet page: http://www.ldschurchnews.com/media/photos/2008/32806.jpg (accessed March 3, 2014). The Masonic/Evangelical angel Moroni was commonplace in early Mormon iconography. "Masonic Moroni," a website that was dedicated to research on Mormonism and Freemason used the weathervane as its banner.

general history contradicts the argument that Mormonism contributed to the resurgence of anti-Masonry in the USA after the famous Morgan affair.[6]

Whenever possible, Mormon temples are built with their main entrance facing East, and they carry the caption "House of the Lord—Holiness to the Lord," phrase which refers as much to Aaron's tiara (*Ex.* 28: 36-37) as to the motto in Royal Arch Masonry. For Mormons, passing the threshold of a temple with that caption is a symbolic passage from "the profane world" into "a sacred space"[7] where they can go through various degrees thanks to instructions and rituals, just like in Old Testament practices and in Masonry.

The association of Christian and Masonic elements has not been a matter of mere display in the Mormon Church's continuing quest for greater recognition and acceptability. They are markers of a genuine syncretism between religion and an esoteric practice and the essence of the Church's rituals. Because of their Masonic nature, those rituals have been in many ways the object of interrogations. This paper addresses one

such interrogation, namely the inclusion of women in Mormon Masonic rituals and practices that are ordinarily the provinces of men. In the following four-step study, we will provide an overview of the historical origins of Mormon temple rituals, before considering the "how" and "why" of the inclusion of women. In the third part, we will take a closer look at the condition of women in Mormon theology and culture in an effort to further explain the role of women in the afore-mentioned rituals. This will lead to the final and last part where we consider the evolution of women inclusion in the Mormon Church in general.

I. A Context Favorable to the Inclusion of Women in Mormon temple Rituals

The date of March 15, 1842, is a historical landmark in Mormonism and in American Masonry. On that day, Abraham Jonas, then Grand Master of the Grand Lodge of Illinois,[8] acted on an official communication filed by Mormon Masons through Bodley Lodge #1 and installed with great pomp and ceremony a lodge in Nau-

---

[6] For an official source, see the scanned-copy published by the Church on the following Internet page: http://www.ldschurchnews.com/media/photos/2008/32806.jpg (accessed March 3, 2014). The Masonic/Evangelical angel Moroni was commonplace in early Mormon iconography. "Masonic Moroni," a website that was dedicated to research on Mormonism and Freemason used the weathervane as its banner.
Alain Bauer is the second Masonic authority in France who has tried to connect Mormonism to anti-Masonry. He stated in an interview to a major French newspaper that "Captain Morgan [was] a Mormon who had left Freemasonry to denounce it" (Koch 2009). Bauer may have erred after having read the title of the article "The Mormon Baptism of William Mormon" (Thompson 1985). But the author of the article indicates from the outset that Morgan "became one of the first persons to receive *by proxy* the new Mormon rite of Baptism for the Dead in the year 1841" (italics added). We know that Morgan went missing in 1826. So, he could not have been made a Mormon in 1841. What we need to understand by the Mormons' baptism "by proxy" is a ritual performed *in absentia*, which they did for a lot of people, including the Founding Fathers, victims of the Holocaust, etc., hoping that this "act of faith" will help save them in the hereafter. Those so baptized are not listed on the Church's membership records.

[7] Mircea Eliade gives a very clear and concise explanation of the difference and interconnection between these two worlds in the first three chapters of *The Sacred and the Profane* (1987).

[8] The Grand Lodge of Illinois had itself been reorganized on April 6, 1840. Abraham Jonas, who was then a Past Grand Master of the Grand Lodge of Kentucky, was voted in as Grand Master of the newly reorganized lodge (Hogan 1969).

voo, Hancock County, Illinois. The town had been created some 10 years earlier by Mormon settlers. We learn in the *Annual Proceedings of the Grand Lodge* held in October of that same year that Jonas installed the following Mormon Masons as presiding officers of the lodge: "George Miller, Master; John D. Parker, S[enior] W[arden]; and L[ucius] N. Scovill, J[unior] W[arden]."[9] It is not indicated in the proceedings, but we also know that John C. Bennett, the second most important leader in the Mormon Church at that time, was made Secretary of the lodge.[10] He was among those who had convinced Jonas to grant the dispensation.

Another significant event that took place on March 15th was the initiation of Joseph Smith, Jr. (1805–1844), the prophet-founder of Mormonism. Two days later, Jonas used his Grand Master prerogative and raised Smith *at sight* to the sublime degree of Master Mason. Obviously, the 24 hour period or so that separated Smith's initiation and elevation does not explain the knowledge he soon displayed of Masonry and of its rituals. His embrace of the Masonry consequently tells us more about his making effectual a link that must have existed between Mormonism and Freemasonry before 1842. Mervin B. Hogan—a Mormon and a Mason who passed away in 1998 but who remains an undisputed authority on matters relating to Mormonism and Freemasonry[11]—declared in a communication to his *Southern California Research Lodge* that "for some fifteen years prior to his accepting and embracing Freemasonry personally in Nauvoo Lodge… Joseph Smith, Jr. was well-informed and thoroughly conversant as to the true character—the basic concepts, principles and goals—of the Ancient Order."[12]

---

[9] *Proceedings of the Grand Lodge of Illinois* (Jonas and Grand Lodge of Illinois 1842, 52). See also the "Freemasons and the Mormons at Nauvoo" (Hogan 1969) for a summary of the proceedings and for a complete transcription of the Dispensation granted to Miller on October 15, 1841, by Grand Master Jonas.

[10] It was discovered later on that Bennett's was not the type of man the Masons, Mormons, and Illinois political circles wanted to mingle with. He had been expelled from Pickaway Lodge, in Ohio, and, at the request of Grand Master Jonas, he was tried in the Nauvoo Lodge for the following grave charges: "*1st Seduction*. For seducing certain previously respectable females of our city by using Joseph Smith's name as one who sanctioned such conduct. *2nd Adultery*. For illicit intercourse with various females frequently. *3rd Lying*. In using Joseph Smith's name as before stated, saying that said Smith taught and practiced illicit intercourse with women, he knowing it to be false. *4th Perjury*. In swearing that he was under duress when he made a certain affidavit before Esq. Wells when it is well known he never was under restraint or confinement at all while in this city. *5th Embezzlement*. For making use of money belonging to the lodge without either knowledge or consent of said lodge. *6th For illicit intercourse with a Master Mason's wife*". It was consequently "Resolved, That John C. Bennett be expelled from this [Nauvoo] Lodge and from all the privileges of Masonry." See "Secretary John Cook Bennett of Nauvoo Lodge" (Hogan 1968), "The Confrontation of Grand Master Abraham Jonas and John Cook Bennett At Nauvoo," a three-part paper presented before the Society of the Blue Friars and subsequently published by the *Pilalethes* (Hogan 1976). Bennett went on to pursue an anti-Mormon career by publishing several exposés of the Church's rituals.

[11] Mervin B. Hogan "Papers" are available at the Special Collections at the Marriott Library, University of Utah, in Salt Lake City (http://content.lib.utah.edu/cdm/ref/collection/UU_EAD/id/1786). Greg Thompson—whom the author of this paper has been privileged to befriend—jealousy guards the "Masonic Collection" they house there, including the papers of Kent Logan Walgren (http://content.lib.utah.edu/cdm/ref/collection/UU_EAD/id/1231), who unfortunately did not live to see the published version of his lifetime work, *Freemasonry, Anti-Masonry and Illuminism in the United States*, 1734–1850 (Walgren 2003). All URLs in this note have been accessed April 3, 2014.

[12] Mervin B. Hogan, "Utah Masons among the Mormons" (Hogan 1993).

The "prior" in Hogan's statement was a way to remind his audience that the roots of the Mormon Church ran deep into a soil that was as much Evangelical revivalist as Masonic. Smith had indeed been immersed in the Masonic environment that prevailed in the East of the USA in the 1820s: he was about 20 years old when the Morgan affair broke out on September 12, 1826; and he was living in Palmyra, a town located at about 50 miles from Batavia, the epicenter of the affair. Clyde Forsberg postulates that "[p]erhaps Smith became a Mason in 1830 and kept it a secret" (2004, 45). According to him, the anti-Masonic context that prevailed in the aftermath of the Morgan supports his hypothesis, and Mormonism's habit of blurring the line between sacredness and secrecy – especially when it comes to temple worship (Mayer 1991; Mauss 1987) – authorizes such suspicion. However, Forsberg also admits in the same breadth that "[n]o record of such an initiation (before 1842) has ever been found." We know that some lodge records had been burned but it makes no doubt that had Smith ever become a Mason in 1830, he would have written or talked about it to his family and associates just like he did about any other significant thing that transpired in his life. Nor have we found any record showing that the prophet-founder of Mormonism ever met William Morgan personally; let alone

Rob Morris' claim that Morgan ever "had been a half way [sic] convert of Joe Smith, the Mormon" or that Smith ever taught him "to see visions and dream dreams" (Morris, 196).[13] Still, it is more than likely that the 20-year-old Smith had access to the abundant literature which divulged Masonic rituals during the Morgan affair. Beside immersion in the general context of the Morgan affair, there is in fact a very tight connection between Joseph Smith and William Morgan: a woman who goes by the name of Lucinda. (The reader is warned though that that story can be very confusing.)

After reporting on the predicament the "poor widow Morgan" found herself with two children, Morris goes on to quote "an amusing notice of [her] marriage" that appeared in the *American Masonic Record*, with editorial comments. The quotation reads:

> The Question is Settled! Anti-Masonry is no more! Since the election it has received a fatal blow; it is dead: Mrs. Lucinda Morgan, the afflicted widow of Captain William Morgan, is married! This celebrated woman who, like Niobe, was all tears and affliction, whose hand was ever held forth to receive contributions from the sympathetic Anti-Masons, who vowed eternal widowhood, pains, and penance, is mar-

---

[13] Morris' suggestion that Joseph Smith almost converted William Morgan is a misleading anachronism. As mentioned above, the Mormon Church officially came into existence in 1830. The *Book of Mormon*, where the names "Mormon" and "Mormonism" actually come from (Arrington 1970), was published that same year. Morris was apparently writing from hearsay—he begins his paragraph with "it was reported to us that," and there are other hints afterwards that support this assumption—but it is still difficult to understand why he should own such a historical gap by publishing it. Homer has suggested that it was "most likely based on the author's attempt to further blacken Morgan's reputation by associating him with the Mormon prophet" (Homer 1994, 19). If such was the case, then we will have seen the exact reverse with Roger Dachez who describes Joseph Smith as "a fellow—much like William Morgan—with a temper, an alcoholic, and of a low level of education…" (Dachez 1992). Smith can be blamed for many things but certainly not for alcohol or a bad temper. Bushman (1988) is an excellent read into the character of the founder of Mormonism and its emergence.

ried! Is married, and, tell it not in Gath, married to a Mason! Behold:-'MAR-RIED. In Batavia, on Tuesday last (November 23, 1830), by the Hon. Simeon Cummings, Mr. Geo. W. Harris to Mrs. Lucinda Morgan, widow of the late Captain William Morgan'.[14]

Morris further writes that Lucinda Morgan Harris and her new husband "moved westward" (278). The couple's westward movement—together with Morgan's two children, to answer Morris' question about them[15]—was not for a honeymoon: it took place in 1834, shortly after the family's conversion to Mormonism. Their destination was Missouri, and eventually Illinois, where Lucinda became one of Smith's polygamous wives[16] in 1838 (Brodie 1945, 436).[17] When Smith died in 1844, Lucinda

was seen "weeping over his body, holding an open copy of Stearns' anti-Masonic treatise" (Homer 1994, 24). Of course, all of that took place years before Lucinda "joined the (Catholic) Sisters of Charity" as Morris has documented (Morris 1883, 278).

Smith did not learn anything from the Harrises that could have made him "thoroughly conversant as to the true character" of Freemasonry as Hogan puts it. But besides them and the anti-Masonic literature that was in print, we know that he had other occasions to discover Freemasonry in much more positive terms through immediate family members who had been long-time Masons. Such was the case of his father, Joseph Smith, Sr.[18]—who briefly shared the same prison cell as Eli Bruce, the Mason and Niagara County sheriff scapegoated for the abduction of William Morgan.[19] He became

[14] Morris, 276-277. As quoted in original.

[15] "I have never learned what became of the two children, one born in 1824, the other in 1826" wrote Morris (279). The names of those children, Lucinda Wesley Morgan and Thomas Jefferson Morgan, have also been located in the records of the Mormon Church. See note 29 in Thompson's "The Mormon Baptism of William Morgan" for the specifics.

[16] The Mormon Church proclaimed the doctrine of polygamy only in 1852, in Utah. But we know that it had been practiced long before that by a select number of Mormon leaders.

[17] It is difficult to tell whether their union was consummated or not while Smith was alive. Homer (2014, 234) doubts that Smith and Lucinda were ever "romantically involved," arguing that "there is no record that they were sealed [i.e., 'married' according to Mormon rituals] but he does concur with other historians that their "marriage" was posthumously confirmed in 1846, after Smith's death. What we know for sure is that at the time of their union, Lucinda was still living with her legal husband, George Washington Harris. He had been the Morgans "neighbor below" as a silversmith; and he—as indicated in the American Masonic Record quoted by Morris—was a Mason and in the same Batavia Lodge as William Morgan (Compton 1997, 45; Morris 1883, 277). Lucinda's legal marriage with Harris ended in divorce for "willfully deserting him, and without reasonable cause absenting [her]self for more than the space of three years" (Morris, 278).

[18] Smith, Sr. was initiated on December 26, 1817, in Ontario Lodge #23 in Canandaigua. He became Fellow on March 2, 1818, and was raised on May 7th. The names of three of his relatives appear in the list of active Masons in the 1802 records of the Randolph Federal Lodge #15. For more details, see my entry "Joseph Smith, Père," in *Le Monde maçonnique des Lumières: dictionnaire prosoprographique*, eds. Charles Porset, Cécile Révauger (Charles 2013, 2567-2570).

[19] Smith, Sr. had been incarcerated for "thirty days" in Canandaigua Jail because he could not pay a debt of 14 dollars. One of his sons "found [him] confined in the same dungeon with a man committed for murder" when he went to liberate him. The story is told *in extenso* and in a very panegyric language by Smith, Sr.'s wife (Smith 1853, 160-166). For further reading, see also "The Patriarch and the Martyr: Joseph Smith, Senior and Eli Bruce in the Canandaigua, New York Jail" (Thompson 1983).

disenchanted with Masonry at about the time when his scion, the future founder of the Mormon religion, reached the required age to become a Mason. He did however make sure before that another one of his sons, the well-named Hyram (later spelled Hyrum), became a Mason.[20]

Another point that should not be missed from the above "history detour" is that the Mormon Church was undergoing significant institutional and doctrinal developments when the Masonic lodge was opened in Nauvoo. Mormon men had been organized into ecclesiastical priesthoods and quorums almost from the beginning of the Church. The Nauvoo Lodge provided another opportunity for them to fraternize.

Just at the time when the lodge was being organized, a group of women asked the Mormon prophet for a unifying organization of their own, like the men's. Smith readily accepted the women's suggestion and on March 17, 1842, created a feminine structure called the Female Relief Society of Nauvoo (Richards 1842, 13). The Relief Society's slogan, *Charity Never Faileth*, would emphasize its social and humanitarian nature but Smith did not mean it to be only another female association where Mormon women would meet and discuss matters of interest to them or to perform subsidiary welfare tasks. In spite of its name, Smith envisioned the Society as a counterbalance, a way to bring Mormon women on an equal footing with men in terms of accessibility to the soteriological rituals of Mormonism. Some of those rituals—washing and anointing, for instance—

had been introduced as early as 1836 (Buerger 2002, 11), but the most significant part of them were still being elaborated when the Nauvoo Lodge was installed.

It should also be noted, for the chronology, that the organization of the Society came about two days after Smith was raised to the sublime degree of Master Mason. And, of all places, the inaugural meeting took place in what Mormons then called the "Lodge Room", above Joseph Smith's store in Nauvoo. The place actually served as the temporary temple of the Nauvoo Lodge until the completion of a Masonic Hall. The Mormon prophet chose his wife, Emma Hale Smith, as president of the Society; two other women were designated to be her councilors. Of particular interest to us is the fact that beside that of "President," Smith gave his wife the title of "Elect Lady." As the Mormons understood it, the title had more to it than a mere biblical reference.[21] It also shed light on Joseph Smith's intentions as to the future of the newly created Mormon women Society, a future that would unquestionably be Masonic. As Michael W. Homer has reminded in a much-celebrated monograph on the similarities between Mormonism and Freemasonry, the reference to the "Elect Lady" existed as a degree in the "French Adoptive Rite which admitted women as early as 1774" (Homer 1994, 29). Homer specifies that the title was also "used as the name of the fifth degree in the adoptive ritual of Eastern Star in 1868" in the USA (*Ibid.*).

Joseph Smith's further inaugural remarks to the Mormon women are also of

---

[20] Hyrum was introduced by his father at Mount Moriah Lodge #112. He was initiated in 1827, but we unfortunately do not have the details of his (Hyrum) initiation and elevation. Hogan notes that his "personal record is lacking Masonic details which were doubtless lost or destroyed due to the Morgan panic" (Hogan 1993).

[21] See 2 John 1:1. The King James Version and the *Bible* of Jerusalem both use the phrase "unto the *elect lady*" (italics added). Instead, the French Louis Second *Bible* identifies the lady as "Kyria". Its reads "à Kyria, l'élue" (to Kyria, the elect).

interest. He instructed the eighteen women in attendance to "not injure the character of any one [and that] if members of the Society shall conduct improperly, [to] deal with them, and keep all your doings within your own bosoms, and hold all characters sacred" (*Op. cit.* 10). His instructions to the women would become more Masonic as time went on. In a meeting held on March 30, he declared that the Society was an "Institution" and that its

> rules must be observed—that none should be received into the Society but those who were worthy—[he] propos'd that the Society go into a *close examination of every candidate*[22]—that they were going too fast [and] that the Society should grow up *by degrees…* that there must be decision of character aside from sympathy—that when instructed we must obey that voice, observe *the Constitution* that the blessings of heaven may rest down upon us—[that] all must *act in concert or nothing can be done*—that the Society should move *according to the ancient Priesthood* [sic], hence there should be a select Society separate from all the evils of the world, choice, virtuous and holy—Said he was going to make of this Society a kingdom of priests as in Enoch's day (*Ibid.*, 22; italics added).

The phrase "Ancient Priesthood" meant the same to Smith as "Ancient Order" or "Masonry." This Masonic intent is finally confirmed in a correspondence in which he wrote to the women of the Society:

> […] there may be some among you who are not *sufficiently skill'd in Masonry as to keep a secret…*. Let this Epistle be had as a private matter in your Society, and then *we shall learn whether you are good masons* [sic] (*Op. cit.* 88).

It shows nowhere, neither in the notes of the Society nor in any other known records of the Mormon Church, that the Mormon women were ever made Masons. But the language used could have been no coincidence or vocabulary mistakes on the part of the six signers of the epistle—Hyrum Smith, Heber C. Kimball, Willard Richards, Vinson Knight, Joseph Smith, and Brigham Young—all of them Masons.[23] Yet, the passage we have quoted from the epistle triggers several questions: How could the Mormon women have learned to be "skill'd in Masonry" and to be "good Masons" if they had never been initiated or somehow been taught the principles of Masonry? Could Smith and his associates have initiated them secretly, without proper authorization, and without recording the event? Whatever the

---

[22] The Society did actually create "[a] Committee […] to inquire into the cases of those persons to whom objections were made" to prevent them from participate in its proceedings (*Ibid.*, 34-35).

[23] Interestingly, the first two signers on the list (Hyrum Smith and Heber C. Kimball) had been longtime Masons. Kimball, in particular, had a firsthand experience of the Morgan affair: he had been made a Mason in 1823, Victor Lodge #303, Victor, Ontario County, New York. According to his biographer, "The year following himself and five others petitioned the chapter at Canandaigua, the county seat of Ontario County, for the degrees up to the Royal Arch. The petition was favorably considered, but before it could be acted upon the Morgan anti-mason riot broke out, and the Masonic Hall, where the chapter met, was burned by the mob and all the records consumed". Kimball is quoted saying that he "[had] been driven from [his] houses and possessions, with many of [his] brethren belonging to that fraternity, five times" but he was pleased to report that he had been "as true as an angel from the heavens to the covenants [he had] made in the lodge at Victor" (Whitney 1888, 26-27).

answers may be, the Masonic references leading to the epistle, together with the rituals in the Nauvoo temple of the Mormon Church, show that for the Mormons, the Female Relief Society of Nauvoo was the female Masonic counterpart of the male Nauvoo Lodge and of the Church's male priesthood. This explains why Smith declared "The [Mormon] Church was never perfectly organized until the women were thus organized."[24] Indeed, Perfection, as the term is understood in Mormon theology, could not be attained without the women.

In May 1842, about three months after the Mormon prophet became a Mason, and after the organization of the Female Relief Society of Nauvoo, he revealed to his followers a ritual called "Endowment." It was a much expanded version of the rituals of washing, anointing and of laying on of hands; so much so that those rituals soon became known as "initiatory" or "preparatory ordinances" to the "endowment." The new ritual was introduced about four years before the Mormon temple in Nauvoo would be completed. As a consequence, the ceremony was at times performed in the "Lodge Room." This situation, together with Joseph Smith's teachings, further blurred the line between Mormonism and Masonry. Heber C. Kimball was among those who heard him preach on the "similarity of preast Hood [sic] in Masonary [sic]."[25] And Brigham Young recalled the ceremony instituted by Smith in the following terms:

> [...] we got our washings and anointings under the hands of the Prophet Joseph Smith at Nauvoo... and had

our garments placed upon us and received our New Name. After he had performed these ceremonies, he gave [us] the *Key words*[,] *signs, tokens* and *penalties...* with the *key words pertaining to those signs.*[26]

Prior to the introduction the "endowment," the situation of Mormon women was strictly identical to that of other women in other religious groups in nineteenth century America. Unless such women could come up with prophetic claims as Mother Ann Lee had done a few decades before the emergence of Mormonism, it was very unlikely for them to receive and to officiate in sacred rituals on an equal footing with men. Some actually abhorred the very idea of women praying in public. Peter Cartwright, the revival preacher, wrote that "there [had] been fashionable objections to females praying in public" in his early days in the Methodist Episcopal Church (Cartwright 1857, 517). Charles Grandison Finney, the most famous Congregational thinker of the second Great Awakening, himself a former Mason, was roundly criticized by Lyman Beecher and Asahel Nettleton on the matter of women praying, insisting that "when on accounts of great judgments, it was enjoined on females to pray, it was the wife apart, and the husband apart"; (p. 89) otherwise, "female prayer in promiscuous (public) assemblies for worship [was] expressly forbidden", less they lose "some portion at least of that female delicacy..." (1828, 89-91). In this nineteenth century context, the introduction of the Mormon "endowment," which we will now consider, was a little revolution.

---

[24] LDS Church Educational System 1993, 248.

[25] Heber C. Kimball to Parley P. Pratt, 17 June 1842, Parley P. Pratt Papers, LDS archives; quoted in Homer 1994, 68.

[26] Journal of L. John Nuttall, February 7, 1877; quoted in Buerger 2002, 39. Our emphases.

II. "Sisters" at Church and "High Priestesses" in the Mormon Temple

As already stated, once a Mormon temple is dedicated, only members "in good standing," that is, those who have been baptized for at least one year and who hold a pass, or "temple recommend," have access to its precincts.[27] There, they can receive and administer in what Mormons consider as their most sacred ceremonies.

Once inside the Mormon temple, men and women take part in the same rituals and receive the same instructions; although they are assigned to separate quarters for the initiatory, or preparatory, rituals. The revolution for Mormon women lies in this: contrary to regular Mormon "church rituals," it is the "Sisters"—except in one case which we shall see later on—who officiate as "High Priestesses" in administering the rites to each other. The term of "High Priestess" is used by some Mormon feminists to echo the fact that to officiate in the "initiatory ordinances" and in the "endowment," a Mormon male must be a "High Priest" in the Melchizedek Priesthood.[28]

a. Mormon "Initiatory Ordinances" or Preparatory Rituals

When a female recipient participates for the first time in the rituals of the Mormon temple, she is accompanied by another "Sister" who is familiar with the rituals and temple procedures. The recipient passes through a cabin where she frees herself from her worldly clothes, jewels, etc. She puts on a white cloak, opened on both sides, and goes to the initiatory area of the temple. There, she meets two female officiators who symbolically wash her with water, and anoint her with pure olive oil. The officiators say a special prayer and then clothe the recipient in a white undergarment that has, among other symbols, a square and a compass on the top left and right, respectively. They instruct the recipient on the symbols and the need to wear the undergarment for the rest of her life.

After the preparatory rites, the recipient goes back to the cabin where she dons a white robe. Her guide then takes her to the next step which is the "endowment" *per se*. On her way to the endowment area, the recipient is given "a new name" in accordance with some biblical references (cf. *Rev.* 2:17; *Isaiah* 62:2) and is instructed not to divulge it to anyone, except at such appropriate location and time forward. The reception of the "new name" is symbolic of the recipient's birth into her new life as an "endowed" (initiated?), a life that she will discover in several stages (degrees?) during the ritual. But the secrecy around the "new name" is more a matter of principal: it is the same entrusted to all the every female recipients in any given day. This could be explained by the fact that in the endowment ceremony, all the female recipients

[27] The "temple recommend" is a certificate that comes in the form of a card. It is signed by two ecclesiastical authorities after individual interviews, and it testifies to the bearer's moral worthiness and belief in the Godhead, in the divine origins of Mormonism, etc. Once delivered, the card is valid for two years, but it can be suspended at any time in case of disqualification. Baptized teenagers from 12 years old on, and new concerts who have not met the one-year membership requirement, can still go to the temple to perform baptisms by proxy or "baptism for the dead."

[28] Mormon males who are 18 or older are "ordained" to the office of "Elder," but this ecclesiastical office does not give the authority to administer the rituals under consideration.
The Aaronic Priesthood is the second and lowest priesthood rank in the Mormon Church.

symbolically become "Eve" and the males "Adam." After they have received the preparatory rituals and the new names at different ends of their temple, Mormon males and females congregate to the room where they begin the endowment *per se.*

b. The "Endowment"

Brigham Young (1801–1877), Joseph Smith's charismatic, who also became a Mason in Nauvoo in 1842,[29] once defined the endowment ceremony as follows:

> Your *endowment* is to receive all those ordinances in the House of the Lord, which are necessary for you, after you have departed this life, to enable you to walk back to the presence of the Father, passing the angels who stand as sentinels, being enabled to give them the key words, the signs and tokens, pertaining to the Holy Priesthood, and gain your eternal exaltation in spite of earth and hell.[30]

Thus, starting with the first meaning of the word endowment, the ceremony consists in giving a ritualized, metaphorical "dowry." It is transmitted by the passing of knowledge, of signs and of symbols, both through gestures and physical contacts such as handshakes or the reception of special undergarments—as we have seen it. The reception of such a dowry is deemed essential to the recipient's salvation in the hereafter. The "knowledge" dispensed in the ritual is taught in the form of a drama of life's journey, according to Mormon understanding of the notion of "Life." This journey is made

of three major stages: it begins in a pre-terrestrial life, moves to the Earth's stage with Adam and Eve and their transgression in the Garden of Eden, etc., and it continues to a post-terrestrial life.

Contrary to the initiatory ordinances, in the different stages of the endowment, male and female are seated respectively on the right and left sides." The full ritual is meant to prepare recipients to become "Kings and Priests" and "Queens and Priestesses" in God's Kingdom. The main officiator in the ritual is a High Priest in the Mormon Melchizedek Priesthood, and he is assisted by a "Sister" who officiates with the same authority when comes such time during the ritual when they both have to administer the "signs and tokens" and show the recipients, according to their sex, how to perform them properly.

During the first stage of the endowment, our female recipient is shown a drama whose highlight is Adam and Eve's transgression as recounted in the book of Genesis. At this stage, the recipient puts on a green apron, a symbolic representation of the fig leaves worn both by Adam and by Eve to cover their nudity before their banishment from the Garden of Eden. The female recipient (as does the male) receives some more instructions and then the first signs of the "Aaronic Priesthood," together with their respective names. She commits never to reveal them outside of the temple. She also makes a number of clothing manipulations: she covers her head with a thin white veil (the men wear a white beret); wears a white roman gown above her white robe; ties a ribbon around her waist with the knot on the left; ties back her apron;

---

[29] According to Hogan (1993), Young was initiated as an Entered Apprentice on April 7, passed Fellow on April 8, and was raised on the April 9, 1842.

[30] *Journal of Discourses* 2, p. 31 (Young 1856); quoted as in original.

and, lastly, she puts on a pair of white slippers. Once she has donned all the above accoutrements (with the help of her "guide"), the recipient is ready to receive "the first sign of the Melchizedek Priesthood," a special grip, and to proceed to the second phase of the endowment ceremony. This second phase usually takes place in a different room. In the Church's temple in Salt Lake City, progression through the stages of the ceremony is materialized by a symbolic ascension to a room situated higher than the previous one. It is also one of the two temples where the recipient actually sees a live performance of the "life's journey" drama.

The recipient receives several signs and symbols of the Melchizedek Priesthood in the second phase of the endowment, and she makes other clothing manipulations, the most meaningful being to tie the knot of her ribbon on the right. She is also given the second sign of the priesthood, but she will not know its name only when she is deemed ready to obtain "more light" or the knowledge necessary to pass a curtain that symbolizes the separation between the terrestrial and post-terrestrial journeys. At the convenient time, the "High Priestess" leads her to the veil behind which stands a male officiator—and this is the only exception where the person administering to the women in the Mormon temple is not a female. The officiator represents the "sentinels" who guards the gates of Heaven, as implied in Brigham Young's definition of the purpose of the endowment (quoted above). The "High Priestess" announces the recipient by knocking with a mallet. When the officiator manifests himself, the female officiator introduces the recipient by the name of "Eve" and states the reason of her presence at the curtain. At the request of the officiator, the recipient gives her own "new name," performs all the signs and tokens of the Aaronic and Melchizedek Priesthoods and identifies them by their individual names, as far as she knows them.

Of course, when she is asked the name of the "second sign of the Melchizedek Priesthood," the recipient states that it had not been disclosed to her and that she had come to the curtain to receive it. To obtain the name, the recipient and the male officiator face each other through the curtain, using special Masonic-shaped openings that allow them to place their left hands on each other's left shoulders and to clasp their right hands in a particular grip. The officiator whispers the name of the sign to the recipient who then satisfactorily goes over all the signs, tokens, and names of the two priesthoods before being admitted to the officiator's side of the curtain. The passing of the curtain marks the end and second stage of the endowment and stands as a symbolic admission into the presence of God. Accordingly, the room of the third stage, the "Celestial room," is a very sumptuous and quiet place where the recipient can meditate.

c. Masonic Initiation or Mormon "Endowment"?

Some changes have been introduced over time in the way the Mormon ritual is performed, but its core and the principle behind it have remained the same. Anyone familiar with Masonic initiation will have noticed the striking similarities between the few elements we have mentioned of the signs, tokens, language, etc., of the Mormon endowment and the three-degree initiation in Craft Masonry. Those similarities and the chronology of events—installation of a Masonic lodge in Nauvoo, initiation of the first and succeeding Mormon prophets, etc.,—lead us to wonder whether the Mormon women (and Mormons in general) who have been to the temples of their Church are "endowed" or "initiated" as into a parallel form of Masonry.

Michael T. Griffith, a Mormon scholar and apologist, has suggested that the similarities do not necessarily make the Mormon rituals a Masonic initiation. For him, the question has to be viewed in the larger context of group interaction followed by inevitable syncretism or transposition. He argued that early Christians borrowed from the iconographic pantheon of pagan nations to construct their own religious culture, and he illustrated his point with the example of the "Good Shepherd" that is considered as a Christian iconography but which was an early pagan symbol of humanitarian concern and of philanthropy.

The answer as to whether Mormon ritual is a Masonic initiation is obvious when considered from the standpoint of the Mormon Church: it does not make any such claim. The matter is also easily settled when the Mormon ritual is considered in light of its Masonic "regularity." Still, Smith's Masonic "Brethren" of the *Grand Lodge of Illinois* did not see his ritual as a mere religious ceremony. "Mormon Masonry," as they called the endowment, "soon became a stench in the nostrils of every Craftsman who had any knowledge of it. At the fifth annual communication, October 7, 1844, the thing was banished from our soil."[32] Glen Cook, the first Mormon to

have headed to this day the *Grand Lodge of Utah* since its creation in 1872,[33] has reminded in an interview with historian Kenneth W. Godfrey that the Illinois Masons accused Joseph Smith of having plagiarized the Masonic ritual, of having initiated not only men but, worse yet, women in an authorized lodge (Godfrey 1971, 84).[34] It would take us too far from our subject to investigate in this paper the conflict that resulted between the Mormons and the Masons in Illinois. The tone of the quotation from the Forty-Fourth Communication of the Grand Lodge gives a very good idea of the tensions. So, suffice it to say here that Smith's assassination in 1844 and the subsequent removal of the Mormons to Utah beginning in 1846 were also the results of such conflict.

III. Beyond the Ritual: Mormon Women and *God-the-Mother*

The Mormon ritual was certainly not "regular" from a Masonic standpoint but it allowed women access to rituals in a way that was nonetheless atypical in the nineteenth century American religious landscape. This movement towards more gender equality in Mormonism was not limited to temple rituals. The conver-

---

[31] "Masonry and the LDS Temple": http://www.lightplanet.com/mormons/response/qa/temple_masonry.htm (accessed April 3, 2014). See also "The Message and the Messenger: Latter-day Saints and Freemasonry" from the Mormon apologist Greg Kearney, also a Mason.

[32] *Proceedings of the Grand Lodge of the State of Illinois*, "Forty-Fourth Grand Annual Communication, held at Chicago, October 2, 3 and 4, A. L. 5883," Appendix, p. 39.

[33] Cook was the 2008–2009 Grand Master of the Grand Lodge of Utah. We learn from his official biography page that he has had several important positions in Masonic lodges in Utah as well as in England. See for further detail "Most Worshipful Brother Glen A. Cook" at http://www.utahgrandlodge.org/pgm/pgm-glen-cook.html (accessed April 3, 2014).

[34] Cook, and Godfrey, discussed the connection between Mormonism and Freemasonry in an interview aired as part of the program "Mormons and Masons" by KUTV, a Salt Lake City television station. A very instructive video of the program can be viewed at http://www.youtube.com/watch?v=O7xenoe4sdI (CBS, "Mormons and Masons" [KUTV NEWS] 2011) (accessed April 3, 2014). See also "A Mormon Mason: New Grand Master is the First in a Century Who is LDS" (Moore 2008).

gence of factors such as the encounter between Mormonism and Freemasonry, the organization of the Female Relief Society of Nauvoo, and the introduction of the endowment were all part of the a larger dynamic in the Mormon Church that opened the way for more recognition and which empowered women.

Beside a total administrative control of their Society until the first half of the twentieth century, Mormon women had a journal of their own, *The Woman's Exponent*, which was published in Utah from 1872 to 1914; they had access to medical practices and they participated in social and political activities. Emmeline B. Wells, the Society's president editorialized in first *Woman's Exponent* issue:

> In the application of manhood suffrage a wrong is inflicted upon the women of these United States, as States—one which the women of Utah do not have to bear. While the elective franchise is enjoyed by many foreign born citizens who may be but poorly informed on the exercise of that privilege and by the lately emancipated colored population, millions of intelligent native-born women are deprived of it simply because nature qualified them to become mothers and not fathers of men. They may own property, pay taxes assist in supporting the government, rent their heart-strings in giving for its aid the children of their affections, but they are denied all right to say who shall disburse those taxes, how that government shall be conducted, or who shall decide on a question of peace or war which may involve the lives of their sons, broth-

ers, fathers, and husbands.[35]

"Utah women [did] not have to bear" the suffrage injustice then because the Territorial Legislature had granted them the right to vote in 1870. The U.S. Congress interpreted the Legislature's move as a political maneuver on the part of the Mormon male hierarchy to secure statehood for polygamous Utah. It eventually passed the Edmunds-Tucker anti-polygamy law which disenfranchised all women in Utah in the spring of 1887. Still, when Utah became a State in 1896, Martha Hughes Cannon defeated her husband and became the first state senator in the history of the USA.

Nineteenth and early twentieth century Mormon women also used to perform religious tasks ordinarily done by men such as laying on hands to bless and comfort their children and other women. And, as illustrated in a poem title "Invocation, or the Eternal Father and Mother," they even contributed to Mormon theology. Stanzas three and four, which are of particular interest, read:

> I had learn'd to call *thee* Father,
> Through *thy* Spirit from on high;
> But until the key of knowledge
> Was restor'd, I knew not why.
> *In the heav'ns are parents single?*
> No; the thought makes reason stare!
> Truth is reason, truth eternal
> Tells me *I've a mother there.*
>
> When I leave this frail existence,
> When I lay this mortal by,
> *Father, Mother, may I meet you*
> In your royal courts on high?
> Then, at length, when I've completed

---

[35] "Woman's Rights and Wrongs," *The Woman's Exponent*, June 1, 1872.

All you sent me forth to do,
With *your mutual approbation*
Let me come and dwell with *you*.[36]

The poem is the work of Eliza R. Snow, a nineteenth century Mormon who has been named "Zion's Prophetess," making her a counterpart of Mormonism's first prophet. Her poem carries the alternate title of "O My Father" in the Mormon hymnbook and is sung by Mormons worldwide. We have italicized the archaic personal pronouns "thee" and "thy" to draw attention to the fact that Snow first uses the standard "Our Father Who art in Heaven" form to address a singular, one-person God. The singular pronouns disappear the moment she asks the rhetorical question as to the existence of a Heavenly Mother. From then on, she uses the personal pronoun "you" and prays to a "plural God," plurality of Gods—on which common sense is plain—is composed of her heavenly Parents, that is, a Father and of a Mother.

It could be argued that Snow's poem is but a prayer, an extrapolation, to which some would gladly add "from a heretic mind." Of course, for Mormon women, it means more than that. After the possibility to officiate side by side with men in the Mormon temple, her poem provided her Mormon "Sisters" with a Goddess, a feminine equal to the masculine God, a "God the Mother" to whom they could (and do) relate, a Mother they can even hope to return to at the conclusion of their earthly journey.

Nor is the belief in a female God in heaven only a "women doctrine" in the Mormon Church. The "God the Mother"

doctrine is not something Mormons elaborate upon anymore but it lies deep in the Church's theology. The fact that nineteenth century Mormon prophets accepted Snow's poem and taught the doctrine sheds light on the inclusion of women in the Church. For what is highlighted in the poem is that of "gender," a fundamental and structuring principle in Mormon theology and in the endowment. The ritual, as we have seen it, is accomplished with and around the characters of Adam and of Eve, symbolically represented by each recipient. One may wonder about the reason to use as role models the "First Sinners," especially Eve, who is blamed in certain biblical interpretations as the one who brought about the end of Paradise with all its negative consequences for humanity. The reason is contrary to traditional Christianity, the Mormon Church preaches that the first woman did not "sin" but "transgressed,"[37] that she made *a conscious choice* between two conflicting instructions from God. Indeed, for Mormons, God's first instruction "Be fruitful, and multiply, and replenish the earth, and subdue it..." (*Gen.* 1:28) came in direct contradiction with the one which states "But of the tree of the knowledge of good and evil, thou shalt not eat..." (*Gen.* 2:17). According to Mormon exegesis, it was impossible for Adam and Eve to keep the first commandment since they were in a state of innocence and of ignorance, a state which explains why they were not ashamed of their nakedness (*Gen.* 2:25). If Adam and Eve were not conscious of their physical reality, according to the exegesis, how then could they "be fruitful" and beget children to people the earth?

---

[36] The title of the poem has been changed more than once. It was known as "My Father in Heaven" when it was first published in the Mormon magazine *Times and Seasons* on November 15, 1845.

[37] This subtlety in language appears for instance in one of the Church's 13 articles of faith. The second one reads: "We believe that men will be punished for their own *sins*, and not for Adam's *transgression*." Italics added.

For Mormons, Eve's choice to eat the forbidden fruit made it possible for the couple to acquire the knowledge necessary to work out the first and higher commandment. In other words, had there been no Eve, there would have been no knowledge, no "light." And mankind would have been but "a project" in a monotonous, senseless, unbalanced, and even absurd paradise because Adam and Eve would never have been able to discern between good and bad. The following passage from Mormon scripture preaches that it takes both conditions to make a perfect world:

> For it must needs be, that there is an opposition in all things. If not so [...] righteousness could not be brought to pass, neither wickedness, neither holiness nor misery, neither good nor bad. Wherefore, all things must needs be a compound in one; wherefore, if it should be one body it must needs remain as dead, having no life neither death, nor corruption nor incorruption, happiness nor misery, neither sense nor insensibility.[38]

Mormon exegesis insists further that Adam and Eve were not to be separated and that they continued to be together after their transgression and expulsion from paradise. This gender inseparability also explains why the Mormon Church includes women both to receive and to administer its temple rituals. The inclusion is also a way for the Church to illustrate a key doctrine taught in the staging of the "endowment": from the moment of their transgression, Adam and Eve begin on a long journey throughout which they accumulate knowledge—in the form of signs, tokens, symbols, names, etc. The latter will enable them to return as complete beings to the presence of their Eternal Father and Mother, in whose images they had been created, to paraphrase both Brigham Young and Eliza R. Snow.

IV. Going back to the past?

The Mormon Church has evolved over the years towards the religious and societal American *mainstream*. That has not been without some consequences on the inclusion and role of its female adherents. Surely, its Masonic-like temple rituals and its doctrine recasting Eve in a more positive light (as well as Adam), its claims that Man can work his way to heaven thanks to the endowment, and that there is even a woman next to God, could not be but heresies and misinterpretations for traditional Protestant Churches in the USA. Acceptance into their midst meant that the Salt Lake Church had to change. One of its changes came about in a "revelation" in 1978 authorizing the ordination of Blacks to its priesthood. This revelation ended a practice that dated back to more than a century instituted by, Brigham Young, the most ostensible Mason of the Mormon leaders, who had been adamant that Blacks were *personae non grata* in the Mormon temple because of their supposed Hamitic ancestry.[39]

---

[38] Book of Mormon—2 Nephi 2: 11.

[39] A portrait shows Brigham Young posing in his Masonic jewels on. His views on Blacks were in line with the policy that excluded them from Masonry in the USA. Michael W. Homer argues in his article "'Why then introduce them into our Inner Temple?': The Masonic Influence on Mormon Denial of Priesthood Ordination to African American Men" (Homer 2006) that the exclusion policy in Mormon temples began with Joseph Smith and coincided with the latter's initiation in 1842. We have not found anything in the pre-Brigham Young era, either in statements by the founder of Mormonism or in the ethnic composition of the Church then in support of that argument.

Several other changes, though superficial, were instituted in the Mormon temple rituals in the 1990s. They consisted mainly in the deletion of the Masonic gesture showing the penalty an endowed Mormon was to inflict upon himself or herself should he/she violate his oath never to divulge the particulars of the rituals. But even without the explicit penalty gestures, the core of the rituals still remains very Masonic.

For Mormon women, the changes were far from being superficial. Mormon feminists and intellectuals, especially the historian D. Michael Quinn, have demonstrated that the women's "sphere of influence" has been reduced. It has been limited to the temple rituals and to maternity whereas Mormon men continue to perform ordinary church tasks and to manage the affairs of the institution. The female Society still exists but it has much less autonomy. For Mormon feminists, this current reality is a regression compared to their nineteenth and early twentieth century conditions. They object to being confined to a supposedly nobler status of Motherhood and to the home while men hold the Priesthood and manage the Church, work outside of the home, etc. For them and their supporters, Joseph Smith meant exactly what he had said when it came to empowering women through the temple rituals. Mormon women do not have hands laid on their heads, as is the case for men, to be ordained to priesthood or ecclesiastical positions in the Church's structure as such but they claim to have received the same priesthood power as men by virtue of their endowment.[40] Smith had indeed taught his followers that

> "All priesthood is Melchizedek; but there are different portions or degrees of it. The priesthood bestowed in the temple is the same priesthood given by the laying on of hands, but it is a fullness of that authority and embraces all other authorities, appendages, and offices."[41]

Mormon feminists began to use the endowment case and Smith's statement in the 1970s, and again in the 1980s, to denounce the fact that they were being sidestepped and deprived of their rights to use their priesthood power outside of the temple. To illustrate their willingness to go back to the nineteenth century basics, some of those feminists began to do more than what Eliza R. Snow had intended in her poem by praying to "God the Mother" while rejecting the traditional masculine God. The cover and title of the volume *Women and Authority: Re-Emerging Mormon Feminism* (Hanks 1992) sets the tone of their conflict with the Mormon patriarchal establishment: its illustration is nothing less than a picture of the "Ludovisi Throne" showing the birth of the goddess Aphrodite and her elevation by the two Hours. Aphrodite is a woman-god slightly different from the one imagined by Snow. The book was published at the height of tensions between the intellectuals and the Church. Several of them, including the volume's editor,[42] were excommunicated; a number of others simply left Mormonism

---

[40] See in particular D. Michael Quinn's "Mormon Women have had the Priesthood Since 1843" in *Women and Authority*.

[41] Quoted in *The Words of Joseph Smith* (Ehat and Cook 1980, 59).

[42] After about 20 years, Hanks was eventually readmitted into membership in the Mormon Church at her own request. See "Excommunicated Mormon to tell how she came back to the Faith" (Stack 2012).

of their own free will. The excommunications generated intense opposition from the beginning but the movement eventually lost its momentum as its number of supporters declined.

Several factors can account for the fact that the internal feminist movement did not appeal to a majority of Mormons to demand a restoration of the nineteenth century version of Mormonism. One of them is the fact that Mormon women do not speak as "one woman" in reclaiming their past privileges: the authors of *American Grace* have found that 52% of Mormon men favor the idea of "women as (lay) priests;" it seems however that 90% of Mormon women oppose the idea (Putnam and Campbell 2010, 244).[43] The percentage may be somewhat overblown, but after more than 10 years of research on Mormonism, we have also come to the conclusion that a majority of Mormon women do not really aspire to becoming priests because they feel valued and recognized in the Church's Female Relief Society as it now functions. It still looks very much like the female equivalent of the men's priesthood: the "Sisters" meet every Sunday for religious lessons and to conduct businesses, they have their general conferences as the men do. Still, the Society has been placed under the control of masculine authority throughout the Church. The women who are satisfied with the Society as it is now have no idea of what it was like before because the Church's official publications tell them about the *story* of Mormonism—which emphasizes the social and humanitarian goals of the Society and the need for women to be good mothers and good spouses. The vast majority of such

women may never have been exposed to the non-censured *history* of the Society and how it really relates to the priesthood and to Mormon temple rituals.

The next reason to account for the failure of Mormon feminists to reinvigorate feminism within the Church has to do with the complexity of the Mormon past: the Church in the days of their foremothers was much more inclusive, but those were also the days of polygamy. It did prohibit the practice as part of an effort to allow Utah to become a State in 1896, but the fact that polygamy ever existed in their history makes their Mormon past difficult to come to term with.

The final reason that may be put forward is the fact that in spite of changes in the conditions as "Sisters," Mormon women continue to play the part of Eve in the temple rituals. This role makes the Mormon temple their unassailable fortress: it is virtually impossible for the Church to exclude them or to reduce their role without changing the way the rituals are administered and without renouncing a large segment of its theology.

Conclusion

By instituting the endowment, a soteriological ritual for the Mormons but which is also very Masonic, as we have seen it, Joseph Smith, pitted the new religious movement as a third way between traditional Christianity and Freemasonry. No other religious group in America, which claims to be a part of Christianity, had tried to accomplish that before. The proximity between Mormon temple wor-

---

[43] Putnam and Campbell rely on the Roper Center "Faith Matters Survey 2006" based on a sample of 3,108 people throughout all of the USA. Regrettably, they do not give satisfactory information as to the number of Mormon women interviewed, their age bracket, where they reside, etc. Such information would of course have made the percentage more meaningful.

ship and Masonic rituals is even the more surprising if we consider that the man who founded Mormonism in 1830, and a significant number of his disciples, knew from firsthand experience of the tidal wave that had swept the USA beginning in 1826 that it bore not well to claim Masonic affinity. Yet, by bringing together Freemasonry and traditional religious beliefs, Smith also innovated with a ritual in which the "First Woman" in the Judeo-Christian myth, Eve, is rehabilitated: she is no more the "Great Sinner" responsible for the ills of humanity. It is because of that belief that Mormon women are endowed and empowered with the same authority as the male priesthood of the Church to administer the ritual to their "fellow sisters."

Yet, we have also shown that the inclusion of women in the Mormon Church has its limits. Aside from the temple ritual, there seems to be a "glass ceiling" barring them from participation in the "everyday" ecclesiastical functions of the Church. Strangely, those "everyday" functions are the ones that come with the power and a seat in the Church's "Quorums," the bodies that make the decisions. This situation reveals a major dissonance: on the one hand, Mormon women are fully involved in spiritual temple matters that are not visible to the common man and, on the other hand, they are kept away from the "profane" activities that are seen by everyone. Thus, the Mormon Church warrants the perception that it is mainly a patriarchal institution perpetuating the old model of "woman at home and men at work," a paradoxical situation considering its theological and nineteenth century gender-inclusivity approach.

Selected bibliography

Arrington, Leonard J. 1970. "James Gordon Bennett's 1831 Report on 'The Mormonites.'" *BYU Studies* 10 (3): 353-364.

Beecher, Lyman, and Asael Nettleton. 1828. *Letters of the Rev. Dr. Beecher and Rev. Mr. Nettleton, on the "New Measures" in Conducting Revivals of Religion.* New York: G. & C. Carvill.

Brodie, Fawn McKay. 1945. *No Man Knows My History: The Life of Joseph Smith, the Mormon Prophet.* Second edition, revised and enlarged. London: Eyre & Spottiswoode.

Browning, Daniel L., and Grand Lodge of Illinois. 1883. *Proceedings of the Grand Lodge of the State of Illinois Ancient, Free and Accepted Masons.* Forty-fourth Grand Annual Communication, Chicago, 2-4 October 1883. Freeport, IL: Journal Stream Press and Bindery.

Buerger, David John. 2002. *The Mysteries of Godliness: A History of Mormon Temple Worship.* Salt Lake City, UT: Signature Books.

Bushman, R.L. 1988. *Joseph Smith and the Beginnings of Mormonism.* Urbana and Chicago, IL: University of Illinois Press.

Cannon, Mark W. 1961. "The Crusades Against the Masons, Catholics, and Mormons: Separate Waves of a Common Current." *BYU Studies* 3 (2): 23-40.

Cartwright, Peter. 1857. "Methodist Usages," 515-520. In *Autobiography of Peter Cartwright, the Backwoods Preacher,* eds. William P. Strickland. New York: Carlton & Porter.

Charles, Carter. 2005. "Priesthood and Leadership in the Church of Jesus Christ of Latter-day Saints." Master's thesis. Bordeaux : Université Bordeaux Montaigne.

Charles, Carter. 2011. "Mormonisme et Franc-Maçonnerie: Du rôle des femmes dans les rituels du temple mormon." In *Les Femmes et La Franc-Maçonnerie. Des Lumières à nos jours*, eds. Cécile Révauger, and Jacques Lemaire. Belgium: La Pensée et les Hommes, 281-297.

Charles, Carter. 2013. "Joseph Smith, père." In *Le Monde maçonnique des Lumières: dictionnaire prosoprographique*, eds. Charles Porset, and Cécile Révauger. Paris: Champion, 2567-2570.

Church Educational System. 1993. *Church History in the Fulness of Times*. Salt Lake City, UT: Church of Jesus Christ of Latter-day Saints.

Compton, Todd. 1997. *In Sacred Loneliness: The Plural Wives of Joseph Smith*. Salt Lake City, UT: Signature Books.

Dachez, Roger. 1992. *Sources et histoire de l'antimaçonnisme aux États-Unis*. William Preston: Loge d'études et de recherches. http://www.logenationalefrancaise.fr/ler/wp/57-wp02antimaconnismeetatsunis (accessed March 21, 2013).

Davis, David Brion. 1960. "Some Themes of Counter-Subversion: An Analysis of Anti-Masonic, Anti-Catholic, and Anti-Mormon Literature." *The Mississippi Valley Historical Review* 47 (2) (September 1): 205-224.

Ehat, Andrew F., and Lyndon W. Cook, eds. 1980. *The Words of Joseph Smith*. Provo, UT: Brigham University Religious Studies Center.

Eliade, Mircea. 1987. *The Sacred and the Profane: The Nature of Religion*. Translated by Willard R. Trask. Harcourt Brace Jovanovich.

Forsberg, Clyde R. 2004. *Equal Rites: The Book of Mormon, Masonry, Gender, and American Culture*. New York: Columbia University Press.

Godfrey, Kenneth W. 1971. "Joseph Smith and the Masons." *Journal of the Illinois State Historical Society* 64 (1): 79-90.

Hanks, Maxine. 1992. *Women and Authority: Re-Emerging Mormon Feminism*. Salt Lake City, UT: Signature Books.

Hogan, Mervin B. 1968. "Secretary John Cook Bennett of Nauvoo Lodge." *Philalethes: The Journal of Masonic Research & Letters*. http://www.tntpc.com/252/philalethes/p70aug.html#Secretary%20John%20Cook%20Bennett (accessed March 22, 2013).

Hogan, Mervin B. 1969. "Freemasons and the Mormons at Nauvoo." *Philalethes: The Journal of Masonic Research & Letters* (August). http://www.tntpc.com/252/philalethes/p69aug.html#Freemasons%20and%20the%20Mormons%20at%20Nauvoo (accessed March 22, 2013).

Hogan, Mervin B. 1976. "The Confrontation of Grand Master Abraham Jonas and John Cook Bennett at Nauvoo." *Philalethes: The Journal of Masonic Research & Letters*. http://www.tntpc.com/252/philalethes/p76jun.html#Abraham%20Jonas%20and%20John%20Cook%20Bennett; http://www.tntpc.com/252/philalethes/p76aug.html#GM%20Abraham%20Jonas%20and%20John%20Cook%20Bennett%20At%20Nauvoo.

Hogan, Mervin B. 1993. "Utah Masons among the Mormons." Conference, Southern California Research Lodge. http://www.skirret.com/papers/utah_masons_and_mormons.html (accessed March 22, 2013).

Homer, Michael W. 1994. "'Similarity of Priesthood in Masonry': The Relationship Between Freemasonry and Mormonism." *Dialogue* 27 (3). http://www.mormonismi.net/pdf/homer1994.pdf (accessed April 3, 2014).

Homer, Michael W. 2006. "'Why then Introduce them into Our Inner Temple?': The Masonic Influence on Mormon Denial of Priesthood Ordination to African American Men." *John Whitmer Historical Association Journal* 26: 234-259.

Homer, Michael W. 2014. Joseph's Temples: *The Dynamic Relationship between Freemasonry and Mormonism*. Salt Lake City: University of Utah Press.

Jonas, Abraham, and Grand Lodge of Illinois. 1842. *Proceedings of the Grand Lodge of the State of Illinois Ancient, Free and Accepted Masons*. Proceedings of the Grand Lodge of Illinois at the Grand Annual Communication, Jacksonville, Oct 3-, 1842. Illinois.

Kearny, Greg. 2005. "The Message and the Messenger: Latter-day Saints and Freemasonry." 2005 FAIR Conference, Sandy, UT. http://www.fairlds.org/FAIR_Conferences/2005_Latter-day_Saints_and_Freemasonry.html (accessed October 5, 2010).

Koch, François. 2009. "Dan Brown a une fascination sympathique pour la franc-maçonnerie." *L'Express* (November 27). http://www.lexpress.fr/culture/livre/dan-brown-a-une-fascination-sympathique-pour-la-franc-maconnerie_831225.html (accessed

March 21, 2013).

Mauss, Armand L. 1987. "Culture, Charisma, and Change: Reflections on Mormon Temple Worship." *Dialogue: A Journal of Mormon Thought* 20 (4): 77-86. http://www.dialoguejournal.com/wp-content/uploads/sbi/articles/Dialogue_V20N04_79.pdf (accessed March 29, 2013).

Mayer, Jean-François. 1991. "Du secret dans le mormonisme." *Politica Hermetica* (5) (November 1): 14-30.

Moore, Carrie A. 2008. "A Mormon Mason: New Grand Master is the First in a Century Who is LDS." *Deseret News* (March 29). http://www.deseretnews.com/article/695265549/A-Mormon-Mason-New-grand-master-is-the-first-in-a-century-who-is-LDS.html?pg=all (accessed March 28, 2013).

Morris, Rob. 1883. *William Morgan; Or Political Anti-Masonry, Its Rise, Growth and Decadence*. New York: Robert Macoy, Masonic Publisher.

Putnam, Robert, and David E. Campbell. 2010. *American Grace: How Religion Divides and Unites Us*. New York: Simon & Schuster.

Richards, Willard. 1842. Nauvoo Relief Society *Minute Book: A Book of Records Containing the Proceedings of the Female Relief Society of Nauvoo. Nauvoo*, IL: The [LDS] Church Historian's Press.

Smith, Lucy Mack. 1853. *Biographical Sketches of Joseph Smith the Prophet: And His Progenitors for Many Generations*. Liverpool, England: Latter-day Saints' Book Depôt.

Stack, Peggy Fletcher. 2012. "Excommunicated Mormon to tell how she came back to the Faith." *Salt Lake Tribune*, July 26. http://www.sltrib.com/sltrib/lifestyle/54514350-80/church-excommunicated-faith-hanks.html.csp (accessed December 11, 2012).

Thompson, John E. 1983. "The Patriarch and the Martyr: Joseph Smith, Senior and Eli Bruce in the Canandaigua, New York Jail." *Philalethes: The Journal of Masonic Research & Letters.* http://www.tntpc.com/252/philalethes/p83apr.html#The%20Patriarch%20and%20the%20Martyr (accessed March 22, 2013).

Thompson, John E. 1985. "The Mormon Baptism of William Morgan." *Philalethes: The Journal of Masonic Research & Letters.* http://www.tntpc.com/252/philalethes/p85feb.html#The%20Mormon%20Baptism%20of%20William%20Morgan (accessed March 22, 2013).

Walgren, Kent Logan. 2003. *Freemasonry, Anti-Masonry, and Illuminism in the United States, 1734–1850: Introductory Essays and Entries from 1734 to 1827.* Worcester, MA: American Antiquarian Society.

Whitney, Orson F. 1888. *Life of Heber C. Kimball; An Apostle, the Father and Founder of the British Mission.* Salt Lake City, UT: Juvenile Instructor Office.

Young, Brigham. 1856. "Necessity of Building Temples: The Endowment." *Journal of Discourses* (2), p. 29-33.

www.ingramcontent.com/pod-product-compliance
Lightning Source LLC
Chambersburg PA
CBHW080021280326
41934CB00015B/3428